The Inner Game of Selling . . . Yourself

*Mind-bending ways to achieve
results in business*

JAMES BORG

Mandarin

A Mandarin Paperback
THE INNER GAME OF SELLING . . . YOURSELF

First published in Great Britain 1989
by Heinemann Professional Publishing Ltd
This edition published 1991
by Mandarin Paperbacks
Michelin House, 81 Fulham Road, London SW3 6RB

Mandarin is an imprint of the Octopus Publishing Group,
a division of Reed International Books Limited

Copyright © James Borg 1989

A CIP catalogue record for this title
is available from the British Library
ISBN 0 7493 0840 0

Printed and bound in Great Britain
by Cox & Wyman Ltd, Reading

The Inner Game
of Selling . . . Yourself

James Borg holds a BSc (Econ) degree from the London School of Economics, where he also studied psychology. After leaving university he launched himself on a sales career during which he achieved record-breaking sales and a consistency that was unparalleled. A member of the prestigious Magic Circle, specializing in 'mentalism' (ESP/mind-reading effects), he attributes his success to simply 'getting inside the mind' – something, as the book clearly shows, that we are all capable of achieving. James Borg is also a contributor to newspapers and magazines. As a marketing consultant, he now runs his own company, Borg Marketing Management, helping clients to market their products and services. He lives in London.

*A book for anyone in business
— not just selling.
Knowing how to sell yourself
and how to be able to read people
is essential for us all*

Contents

1 Get inside the mind . . . and you will find . . .   1
2 Mind bending using ESP: Empathy,
    Sincerity, Perspicacity   8
3 Asking questions   14
4 Being a good listener   21
5 Holding attention   31
6 Make your memory pay   50
7 Tricks with the telephone   75
8 Client types   100
9 Stereotype salespeople   115
10 Negotiating to win   125
11 Making words work for you   132
12 Acting the part – wrongly and rightly   140
Questionnaire: have you developed ESP?   166
Answers   177

1

Get inside the mind . . .
and you will find . . .

Salesmanship is not the exclusive province of professional salespeople. Everybody has to put it into practice *all the time*. It's probably better recognized as trying to get other people to do or give something or as trying to get a point across.

Despite all the practice, few perform this art to its best effect. Yet it's so simple. It requires no special skills but just draws upon a few basic personal qualities. The short answer is to 'put *yourself* into selling'.

Every day in offices individuals of varying status in the hierarchy are 'selling' their points of view to others. They may not have the vocation of salesperson but their ultimate aim is the same: getting their viewpoint or message accepted. You see people in discussion, from the boardroom to the rest room, trying to influence one another to agree to a course of action. The successful ones are those who use subtle techniques of persuasion. Their reasoning strikes a chord in the mind of the other(s) and so an idea is accepted.

Now that's salesmanship.

For years there was felt to be something slightly suspect about anybody in the business of selling. This label seemed to stick particularly firmly to those involved in the area of household goods. But whether the product be a vacuum cleaner or an aircraft engine, the selling process is vital to the economy. The manufacturing companies could not exist unless their salespeople went out and persuaded people to buy. And without buyers, there would be no personnel departments, salary departments, production departments or indeed any departments.

Perhaps the fault lay with the companies themselves. Too much emphasis was placed on employing anybody who was prepared to swot up on features of the product and then letting them loose under the company's banner. No regard was paid to the personality of the salesperson and his ability and/or capacity to sell 'himself' (an ability that seems to evolve if you manage to get in tune with the other person).

In the past employers were no doubt impressed by a candidate's ability as a fast talker. You can still find people who bludgeon their way through their sales presentations. But there's no place for this in today's highly professional environment – where perhaps 'fast listener' would be a better quality.

The message gradually seems to be getting through now. Selling is essentially about appealing to human nature. After all – we're dealing with individuals. The game of selling is therefore an *inner* one played in the minds of the participants. The successful salesperson is the one who uses all his resources to *get inside the mind* of each new prospective client and draw out the information he needs to tailor his proposition into a winning one. At the same time the buyer is made to feel that he has won too. It's all down to subtlety and knowingness on the part of the seller.

It's using the art of gentle persuasion to achieve an outcome that is of mutual benefit. And it's recognizing the workings of what psychologists refer to as the *conscious* and *subconscious* mind.

The fact is that messages are mostly decoded in the buyer's unconscious mind, which tends to interpret things on an emotional level. By carefully choosing the right words to plant in the mind, the seeds are sown for a positive effect. The buyer's conscious mind should automatically accept the ideas put over – and that increases the chances of a sale.

The all-seeing, all-knowing salesperson is aware that outside influences can inhibit the effectiveness of his communication and therefore his sale. He can sense when attention is straying and can recognize the effect that certain interruptions will have on the buyer's concentration. He thus compensates for the effects of major disruptions to his presentation. He readjusts his pace to keep in tune with the other person.

Good salesmanship is the basis of success in all occupations. Even 'professional' people are recognizing the benefits of sales technique: solicitors, accountants, architects, surveyors. These practitioners have always sold their services but have not necessarily regarded themselves as salesmen in the literal sense. So they have mostly been content to offer their services in a passive way. No one would dream of calling a solicitor a salesman; but what's the difference between a solicitor or accountant *in situ* trying to engage a client, in the face of competition, for some conveyancing or taxation work, and a salesman going out to win business for his particular company? Equally plumbers, carpenters, private doctors, electricians, chauffeurs are all in the selling game, whenever they directly offer their services to potential buyers. They have to make the sale first, before any work is done.

So an appreciation of selling techniques is essential for everybody. And, even outside work, the same techniques of handling and understanding people on an everyday social level are fundamental. There's always a need to win over other people for one reason or another in every aspect of life. So the same rules hold good.

Getting inside the mind of the other person is vital. But few people make the effort. If they did, then the results would be outstanding. It only requires a keen awareness. If this comes naturally then you're in a minority – but probably a very successful and content minority in both a business and a social context.

What's the secret?

ESP

This is a variation on the theme of extra-sensory perception. We're talking about mental techniques for getting inside the other person's mind. But this ESP demands different qualities:

E   Empathy
S   Sincerity
P   Perspicacity

Empathy

This is the magic personal quality that is at the root of success in communicating with others. If you've got it – *exploit it*! If you haven't – *develop it*!

What is it? It's putting yourself in the other person's mind; feeling with him; understanding how what you say will affect him; being sensitive to his business problems. It's getting in tune with him.

That means, of course, that you will constantly be tailoring your approach and what you say to different people. Because you're treating them as individuals. They are all different. Your job is to find out what they are thinking and show understanding. Your empathy enables you to spot different types of people and almost get inside their minds to find out what will satisfy them, stimulate them, worry them, inspire them. In short – what factors might or might not lead to their doing business with you.

We're talking about what separates the good salesperson from the mediocre. If you have an impressive knowledge about your product but lack empathy, you certainly won't do as well as somebody who has both.

An understanding of human nature and a curiosity about people is what all this really means. Some people have this innate sense to a very high degree. So they use it – successfully. They're almost able to predict how the other person will react to something. They put themselves on a similar wavelength so they know what to say and *how* to say it.

But if you haven't got it – at least be aware of it. Now develop it.

Sincerity

If you're going to develop empathy then you must show sincerity.

There has always been an instinctive mistrust towards anyone selling anything. It's unavoidable. It is a very old assumption. The salesman is there to offload his product on the unsuspecting buyer – who is often warned to beware.

But what about the salesman who genuinely believes in the benefits of his product, and shows it – sincerely? People can spot true sincerity. It's indefinable; it's just there. You know it when you see it. Because it is heartfelt. It shows in the face, in the eyes.

When you show genuine sincerity – that you actually care about the buyer's requirement or problem – you're elevating yourself to a higher plane. The conversation takes on a different tone; the buyer is more receptive to your questions and tells you more. This helps you steer the discussion in the direction that you want. A certain amount of trust has been established.

Again, if you are a sincere person (it isn't difficult) then it probably comes naturally. If you consider you are sincere but it doesn't seem to come across, then relax; lose yourself in being interested. The onus is on you. Show the buyer that you care about his business by asking relevant questions. Don't imply that everything you have to sell would be good for him. Reject some facets of your package as not being suitable – or cost-effective – for him, if this is the case. Point out what might be drawbacks in some areas as far as he's concerned.

When you show sincerity, the buyer feels confident not only about the sale but also about the *after-sale*. *Fact*: many sales never get off the ground because the buyer, though convinced about the product, is worried about what happens after he has bought. In other words, if there is a problem: the self-assembly desk that won't assemble; the computer system that doesn't quite seem to do what the salesman had indicated. The buyer feels more inclined to buy and more confident in making the purchase if you show sincerity. He feels that you would be fair and helpful in the case of any dispute.

Perspicacity

This is really an ingredient of empathy. It's the part that allows you to see into the other person's mind. It means having insight.

Such keen perception comes not only through applying the mind but also by using the senses – looking and listening. This means that every normal healthy person has the built-in potential for perspicacity.

The problem is that because they're so wrapped up in themselves, many people don't apply it often enough. They may sense something about the person they are dealing with *subconsciously* – but that piece of perception is not *registered* and so is not put to good use. It's not used to further one person's understanding of and rapport with another. In any selling situation that can be a big loss

2

Mind bending using ESP: Empathy, Sincerity, Perspicacity

It's amazing, when you look at the basis on which organizations employ people to sell their products, to find that they invariably concentrate on people's product knowledge. This is usually the first thing companies look for – and most training given concentrates on this too. But scant regard is paid to personality, and within that the most important quality – empathy.

Having empathy enables you to gain perception of the true feelings of the buyer.

Most training is limited to one track, such as: how many programmes the dishwasher has; how many megabytes the PC is capable of handling; the durability of the double-sprung mattress; the battery power of the portable phone. Of course product knowledge is essential. It's a prerequisite. Nobody wants to buy from someone who doesn't know enough about what he is selling. But being in tune with the other person is the secret of winning him over. You have to 'read' the buyer's mind. So why is this fact so often overlooked?

Perhaps the feeling is – either you've got it or you haven't. This is true to some extent. If you have natural empathy then you have a great advantage over most people. But if you don't have it, you can still make yourself aware of other people's feelings and inclinations.

People will rarely come out with what they are *really* thinking or feeling. It's the way most of us are conditioned. It's up to you to get into the other person's mind and see what's really going on. For example:

1   You're in a restaurant. You leave almost all of the main course, having enthused about it when ordering.

The head waiter comes to collect your plates. 'Oh – you're not hungry today, madam?'

'The starter has filled me up.' (Thinks: how could they serve up muck like this in such an expensive restaurant?)

'Dessert, madam?'

2   You arrive at work an hour later. Your daughter was taken ill suddenly and you had to take her to hospital early that morning.

Your boss says: 'Sorry to hear about that. Oh – I need this report completed urgently. Could you stay late tonight and have it ready for me first thing for my meeting?'

You instinctively say 'Yes.' (Thinks: damn – I wanted to get to the hospital by 6 o'clock).

3   You're sitting on a train. The seat next to you is empty, as are three seats opposite you. You have your heavy briefcase perched on the seat.

Somebody comes over and says: 'Do you mind if I sit here?'

You remove your case and answer with a half-smile: 'No – not at all.' (Thinks: of course I mind – there are three empty seats opposite, why the hell couldn't you have taken one of those?)

4   The salesperson has arrived 45 minutes late for a meeting with a prospective client. He didn't phone to say he would be delayed.

'Sorry about the delay, Mr Reed.'

'Well – fortunately I haven't got another meeting scheduled, You're lucky.' (Thinks: rude of you not to at least phone to tell me you'd be late. Make it snappy because now I'm not interested in what you've got to say.)

What's worrying in all of these instances is one person's failure to dig deeper and read the other's thoughts. You, as the one who wants something, must be prepared to do the excavation work. You know that you are not going to be helped along with a clear exposition of the buyer's reservations, or his reactions to what you have to offer. But the 'tape drives' are working away inside the brain-computer. It's up to you to probe with your ESP (empathy, sincerity, perspicacity) and get through to the other person in order to further your cause.

Reading people effectively in business situations is the key to individual success. An affinity with people is the common denominator of many accomplished business personalities. They positively enjoy meeting new people.

Meeting people

It's a situation we all encounter every day. Meeting people we know, new contacts, strangers on the train, acquaintances made on holiday. You'd think that doing it so often, we would find it easy and enjoyable. After all, practice makes perfect – or does it?

Unfortunately not. The problem? Your psyche. It's different from everyone else's.

We all have different values, different perceptions, different opinions, all formulated over the years according to our childhood, our education and our own personal experiences. And it's all there nestling in the subconscious. So everything we hear or see is decoded in our minds, drawing upon that programme otherwise known as the subconscious.

So what? It means that people can interpret things quite

differently. Since most of our time on this earth is spent trying to 'sell' or persuade others to come round to our way of thinking, we have to be sympathetic to different points of view.

That means that our reasoning has to be quite powerful and has to be modified each time, depending on whom we are talking to and what we are discussing. The successful person has to call forth quite a repertoire of feelings and emotions to deal with all the different types of people. We have to sell ourselves each time we come into contact with people. It's not a convenient one-off process after which we can lie back for the rest of our lives; it has to be renewed each time.

There lies the problem. We are constantly trying to perfect our image and protect our ego during each encounter. Small wonder that some people absolutely loathe and fear meeting new people.

We are all familiar with that overworked phrase – 'the fear of rejection'. The phrase is a little strong, but the principle is there. It seems to haunt us all, in varying degrees. From childhood we get upset when we ask for things and get turned down. We may sulk. Sometimes this reverses the decision. Other times it results in a sharp smack.

But in business there's no room for sulking. Better not to get turned down at all. How do we minimize refusals? By techniques of persuasion.

For some people the word 'persuasion' has ominous undertones; it implies that something underhand is being effected every time somebody is persuaded to do something. OK, let's line them all up for the pillory:

1 Your secretary, who persuaded you to let her leave work an hour early for a hairdressing appointment (because she'd finished typing your reports on time).
2 Your doctor, who persuaded you to switch to a healthier diet.
3 Your wife, who got you to pay for returfing the lawn.

4   The political party that persuaded you to give them your
     vote.

The paradox is that most people *want* to be persuaded to do
things, to buy things, to make a choice. Deep down we all
hate making decisions. Why? For fear of making the wrong
one. And yet we'll let somebody influence us into *a* decision.
Because we want to reach one.

What we all have an aversion to is the feeling of having
been manipulated. Now that is not good selling.

But this is not what we're discussing here. We're talking
about the art of gentle persuasion. *Subtle* techniques that
work on the mind to produce a desirable result. Good old
harmless stuff.

We're all suckers for courtesy, plain common-sense logic,
sincerity and a host of other emotional feelings that make us
want to deal with somebody. We are convinced by people
displaying these qualities; they will have sold themselves to
us. Having decided that a person is worth dealing with, the
buyer, in any situation, will then be prepared to continue.

What is really going on in the mind is an acceptance of you
as a person. After that your chances are much better. If you
don't pass that first stage – forget it. You have not sold
yourself, and you have reduced your chances of selling
anything else.

Given the choice, we would all like to be able to do
business with somebody we trust and like. Most products
and services are sold in a competitive situation. That is, there
is usually an alternative source. More often than not, if there
is little to choose between different products in terms of
quality and price, we will choose on the basis of the salesman
we would most like to deal with. To repeat – the one who has
sold himself to us.

People will generally not buy something if they are put off
by the salesperson attempting to sell it. This may well be the
case even if they have made up their mind that they want the

product. They will go elsewhere. Just as you, in a selling position, will be assessing the prospect's character, so will he be getting the measure of you. Take a look at yourself. What are you like? Are you easy to get on with or are you abrasive? Is your suit Pierre Cardin or Worzel Gummidge? Is your delivery a dull monotone or do you project enthusiasm? In short – are you an inspiration or are you a turn-off?

Instinctive acceptance of you as a person will ensure acceptance of your *suggestions*. That automatically enables you to be gently persuasive. And that is a potent enough reason to perfect techniques for selling yourself.

3

Asking questions

To get inside the mind you need to master just two fundamentals:

Questioning
Listening

If you think about it logically, it's only by asking questions that you can find out things about people whom you don't know. You seek out their preferences. This can be hard work. And more often than not you have to read between the lines in order to get the true picture.

But so many salespeople think that it is their job to do the talking while the other person does all the listening. That amounts to one-way traffic. Most potential buyers prefer to talk about their business first. After all, the purpose of your visit is to be of help. If you ask questions you can then tailor your presentation to their needs.

Asking the right questions allows you to take several important steps forward:

1   The client feels that you are interested in his business and are not just there to give the hard sell.

2 He is encouraged to give information about his business, which you need to know – especially his problems.
3 You can steer the conversation along the lines you want it to go.
4 You are able to control attention more effectively.

The first six minutes

We are always being told about the crucial first minutes of any sales situation, the first impression stage: what you look like, what you say and what you do. If only this were a fallacy, it would give hope to the slow starters – but these introductory minutes really are make or break.

This is what determines the level of attention you are or are not going to get – whether the client tunes in to your ideas and personality, or switches off. It is rather like scanning through the headlines of a newspaper or looking at the cover or first few pages of a book; you then decide whether to read on. The buyer makes a decision early on: is it worth hearing what this person wants to tell me?

Your line of questioning will establish the effectiveness of the meeting. But many people complain about an uneasiness at the very beginning. They can't get warmed up in the first few minutes, and a stilted atmosphere develops. That is hardly conducive to the rapport we are seeking. The buyer gets bored and feels uneasy because you are ill at ease – the mirror image. He can't wait for you to finish your coffee and wrap everything up. Neither can you.

The problem seems to be this: what to say at the start to somebody you haven't met before. Most people feel uncomfortable. They're so concerned about what they are going to come out with first, that they are in a state of tension. Ironically, this is exactly what is likely to make a mess of their opening words.

What should you talk about: the weather? How bad the traffic was? Should you compliment him on his tasteful choice of mahogany desk? Gaze adoringly at his hopscotch trophy? The answer is – as long as it's *natural*, it doesn't matter. It's the stilted opener (preamble) said for the sake of it and sounding strained and insincere that spoils the mood of the meeting. If what is coming out of your mouth is genuine and sounds it, then go ahead as long as you know when to stop and get down to business.

When meeting a person for the first time, the feeling of discomfort often forces you to say the first thing that comes into your head. Nervousness makes for recklessness. It's as well to remember the old adage that served me particularly well in the classroom: *'Better to keep your mouth shut and be thought a fool than to open it and remove all doubt!'*

Take for instance:

'So good of you to see me, Mr Dean. I'm glad that your company is prepared to let bygones be bygones.' Mr Dean thinks: 'What? I didn't even know my predecessors had ever dealt with this company. I must ask around and see what they fouled up before.'

'Good morning, Mr Dean. The purpose of my visit is to talk to you about our new range. Gladly we've sorted out the problems on the 516 range that you probably read about in the press. Apparently there won't be any legal action now.'

'Sorry I'm late, Mr Dean. Had to sort out a problem with a customer before I left the office. Never rains but it pours. The desks we supplied him with reached him late and then he found that the bases of the drawers were coming away. I daresay it's a simple explanation – the glue probably. Anyway, I'd like to . . .'

These superfluous statements set the meeting off on the wrong footing. If a negative point had emerged naturally (and *subtly*) during the course of the conversation the attitude would probably have been different. The salesman would have had time to sell himself and then present a good company image that could overcome any former bad impression.

Questioning techniques

Certain types of question give us a good psychological insight and so help to bring out other people's thoughts.

The forward question

Here we rely on those good old indispensables: what, why, when, how, where and who.

Remember: these basics are underused by most salespeople, who have a tendency to pussyfoot around and never get to the point. There's a general reluctance to use this direct approach because it can appear too forward. But the correct delivery overcomes this problem.

These are the best questions for getting inside the mind. But the *way* in which they are asked, and the rapport (or lack of) that has already been established, will determine their effect.

Unless you have managed to strike up some empathy, questions like these can be regarded as too direct and an affront to the buyer. They may be interpreted as abrupt and prying, making the buyer feel subordinate to you. But you want him to feel good about himself. The fine balance of the buyer/seller relationship must be struck and held steady.

The secret of getting a good response from forward questions is to prefix with a few words and turn what looks like a prying question into a reasonable one. Consider, for example, these questions and how the alternative version would make the person on the receiving end more receptive to giving the information:

1   'What's your advertising budget for the year?'
    Or:

'Can I ask you – what's your budget for advertising this year?'

2 'Why don't you buy from us anymore?'
Or:
'It would be helpful if we knew why you don't buy from us anymore.'

The key to getting what you want from a direct question is to be courteous; people can't resist it.

The point to be stressed is this. If you can get on the same wavelength as the other person and get him to feel comfortable in your presence – you've done it. You have the scope to ask *direct* questions. That's good for you. You haven't time to waste. He hasn't either.

The attitudinal question

These open-ended questions are designed to draw out a person's overriding interests. For example:

'Mr Dennis, when you talk of wanting to use direct marketing for the campaign, is it the measurement of results that appeals to you most, or what?'

'Tell me, are you concerned more with geographical coverage for the portable phone, or is it the amount of talk time available from the battery?'

'What's your main priority with a folding bed: is it comfort or space saving?'

'How do you feel about using the much lighter and durable plastic material instead of your existing heavier steel?'

The answers you receive to this type of question provide a framework for tailoring the direction of your sales presentation.

The agreement question

Many salespeople, particularly those of the old school (graduates of the 'Academy of Double Glazing and Insurance Salesmen'!) were taught to use questions that get the buyer to answer 'yes.'

Unfortunately, this classic line of enquiry went something like this: 'Am I right in assuming, Mr Fenn, that you'd like to double your profits next year?' Mr Fenn thinks: 'No. I'd like to go bust, idiot!' This kind of moronic question has no place in today's highly professional sales environment. With the hectic pace of business life these day, buyers certainly don't have time to engage in such banter. It's an insult to your client and a poor reflection on you. You're busy too.

Instead, you can profitably ask questions that are *specific* and elicit a response that brings the two of you closer to agreement. For example:

'So, Mr Fenn, getting the right type of people to the seminar is the objective, yes?'

'You want to trim the energy bill with the minimum of disruption to your plant, is that right?'

'You're interested in a maintenance contract that doesn't tie you in for long periods?'

'So you would be happy with a system that could automatically link in to the terminals in your other nine branches?'

The sifting question

Of the various products and services you have put on offer, some may be of interest while others will have been rejected. It's important to sort out the acceptances from the rejections and to *restate* those that have aroused interest. With many meetings running on, the client is unlikely to sustain the concentration to remember exactly what you've said. He forgets. It's up to you to remind him what *he* indicated was interesting.

You're then renewing the discussion on a positive note — on a point that you know has had *impact*. His concentration will now be much better. You may then harness the listener's attention.

Examples of restating are:

'You said, I believe, that overnight accommodation for your delegates is not required. But you would like to discuss a day conference that includes an evening meal?'

'As you said earlier, the smaller fax machines are probably more suitable to your company. Now how about if . . .?'

We assume that the features we consider the most significant about our product are the ones that will most interest the buyer. This is a wrong assumption. People differ widely in their opinion as to what are the most important aspects of a product.

For example, one company buyer of fleet vehicles wants fuel economy, regardless of make, while another wants only a British name. One person buying a vending machine is interested in the range of cold drinks, another buyer is concerned about speed of servicing in the event of break-downs.

You have to probe to find out the purchaser's basic motive for buying. People often don't really know what they want out of something, or have been misguided into focusing on just one aspect of a product

Asking the right questions is our first step to getting inside the mind. Moreover, if our questioning technique is such an important consideration in achieving our goal, then its opposite number — listening — makes for the ideal combination.

4

Being a good listener

When people are accused of being poor listeners it is usually done behind their backs. So they remain unaware of this major failing which can lose them clients as well as friends.

How do *you* rate as a listener? Being a bad one is a very serious sin of which most people are guilty. They only think they listen. The compulsion to speak in very many cases completely devalues the function of listening. Fact: most people prefer talking to listening; and unfortunately they exercise this preference.

It's no good employing your carefully thought-out questioning techniques if you lack the capacity to listen. Chat show hosts like Wogan and Carson, on both sides of the Atlantic, often demonstrate this deficiency. But on the whole interviewers have had to learn to listen to their guests in order to get the most out of an interview.

Active listening is difficult. It requires a lot of concentration. But it has to be mastered. When selling in any situation, listening is probably the most important requirement. Perhaps it's significant that we have two ears and only one mouth!

Nobody could be accused of listening too much. It's surprising what people will tell you if you're a good listener.

Think how it works among friends and acquaintances on a social level.

In business it's no different. People are drawn to a *good* listener. There is a definite appeal in being able to talk to somebody outside the internal politics of their own company who listens objectively. The person bogged down in the red tape of his own position often relishes the therapeutic satisfaction of getting something off his chest to an outsider.

It pays good dividends if you listen. It can establish you as a 'friend'. And that makes for more mutual understanding in the business relationship.

Besides, if you listen carefully you pick up all sorts of information about the idiosyncrasies of the company – and the individual you are dealing with! People who are poor listeners often see listening as a passive – and therefore unproductive – activity. Their *ego* gets in the way. They feel the need to be talking in order to make any impact with the other person.

Observe people in internal meetings and you'll see the talk-talk-talk syndrome with a vengeance. There are those who continually interrupt and engage in superfluous twaddle. It makes them believe that they're contributing. They'll miss important points through butting in. And they'll ask questions to which they already know the answers. But they're communicating, because they're talking. How wrong. Attentive listening is *also* part of communication.

In sales situations you can't afford to monopolize the conversation. Let the other person speak and then, at an opportune moment, you take the reins. It has to be give and take. Talking long and loud doesn't always equate with having personality; it is often a substitute for it.

Productive listening

There's only one way to listen productively: try to remove all distractions from your mind so you can concentrate on the speaker (easier said than done!). Such distractions come from your thoughts, senses and emotions.

For instance, somebody might have just bumped into the back of your car and the nuisance of it keeps coming back to you during your meeting. Or perhaps a noise from the roadworks outside is off-putting. Or you find a painting on the wall particularly absorbing.

What is at the heart of the problem? It is that we can *think* much faster than anyone can *speak*:

1   *Tests have shown that we talk at between 120 and 150 words per minute.*
2   *We think at the rate of around 450 to 600 words per minute.*

Result: since we can think at approximately *four* times the rate that somebody is speaking, we tend to think of other things and not just what is being said.

The implications of this are always evident. When listening to people, the radio, television or whatever, the mind has time to wander away from the words being spoken. So you lose concentration. And if you start thinking about something and it takes you over, you'll blot out the other noise and so switch off. In a meeting situation you may look as though you're listening (to the other person), but you're not actually hearing anything.

So who are you trying to kid when you claim to be a good listener? Listening isn't merely *saying nothing* while the other person is talking. It means *hearing*. And that's what people find difficult.

Because your thoughts formulate faster than somebody's speech, you sometimes want to play word games. There's a strong temptation to finish the sentence for the other person:

'. . . and so I want to avoid any . . .'
   Interruption from salesperson: '. . . further catastrophe.'
'Er – yes. That's right.'

Now, you can do this occasionally but don't make a habit of it. To keep doing it to the same person is not only irritating but is also bad psychology, because the speaker will not feel in control of his own ideas.

Filling in words for somebody on the odd occasion can show that you are actually listening, but it can also mean getting in the way of the other person's ego. It may well look as though you're trying to wrestle original thoughts from him and claim them for your own. That renders you suspect, and is no good for the rapport you're aiming to establish.

But there's another drawback to jumping the gun like this: you can easily guess the *wrong* ending! Perhaps that possibility has never occurred to you, simply because nobody has ever bothered to correct your mistake.

Maybe the client doesn't want to embarrass you and tell you that you're an idiot who has messed up his line of thought. Because he can't do that, he can't continue with his original point (it may have been crucial).

The ending that you so kindly supplied (*i.e. the wrong one*) may put doubts in his mind that never previously existed. For example:

'I'm happy to do business with you – but this time I want to make sure . . .'

Interruption from salesperson: '. . . that you don't get the wrong consignment like you did on the last occasion and then have to wait another three weeks.'

What the client was actually going to say was: 'I want to make sure your company gets paid within 28 days.' (Previously they had taken four months to pay their invoice.)

What's happened now is that the client is alerted to the fact that your company messed up the delivery last time, causing a three-week delay. He may not have known anything about it or may have just forgotten. Now he has doubts because late delivery could cost his company a lot of money. The salesman probably now loses the sale by having thrown in a completely un-thought-out line.

To make matters worse, what the client was actually going to say was to the salesman's benefit.

Another irritating habit adopted by many salespeople is *talking over* somebody else while they are speaking. It's unnecessary, bad manners and damaging to your cause. You're missing out on information which could help you in your sale, while also antagonizing the other person. The other party probably won't tell you this – but he'll think it. And he is unlikely to want anything else to do with you.

If we're really 'listening' then we're picking up more than just the words being spoken. We're hearing the *tone* in which things are said, and observing *facial* expressions and *body* posture. The combination of these observations enables us to *listen between the lines*.

Objections

Most people when challenged in any situation will immediately go on the defensive. When a salesperson is put in this position he must learn to react in a positive way. An inevitable part of salesmanship is facing up to and handling objections. It 'goes with the territory', as they say.

Perhaps the word 'objection', so commonly used in a sale context, is really inappropriate. Many so-called objections are *not* objections at all. They are statements intended as a challenge to try to clear up some doubt or other in the prospect's mind.

Traditionally, most sales training has given prominence to the handling of objections. The result is an almost defensive approach to any question from a customer about the products or services being sold. The salesperson instinctively considers all queries to be objections and so fails to get inside the buyer's mind and work out what he is really saying.

It is important to understand that people do not like making decisions about whether to buy. This is because most buying decisions involve choice. And having a choice means you could have bought another type of the same product (or something else altogether). This inevitably leaves the buyer in some doubt as to whether he has gone for the best option.

But perhaps the heart of the matter is that when we buy something we're usually looking for approval from others. We want reassurance that we've made a wide purchasing decision. We want to hear people say:

'That's a lovely suit you're wearing.'

'That vending machine you had installed really does produce excellent coffee.'

'What a smart attaché case you have: where did you buy that from?'

'The weekend conference you organised at Tylney Hall – good choice!'

When we've bought something, there's usually a partner at home or boss at work from whom we want to secure approval of our purchase.

To try to ensure that we buy wisely, we ask salespeople questions – sometimes awkward ones. They're not *necessarily* objections. They may be questions to help us to be sure in our own mind that this is the right choice; but also we want good selling points to justify having bought something to our boss/partner. In short, we have to 're-sell' the benefits after we've bought it. For example:

'Why did you choose this hotel for our audiovisual presentation? The room hire rate and equipment charges seem much too high.'

To boss: 'Yes, I know that might appear so. But they have technicians on site, so if there's any problem they can be with us in less than two minutes. Also the room is more airy and may prevent too many delegates falling asleep!'

'These mailing lists you've bought work out at £110 per thousand. I can buy lists for £60 a thousand.'

To boss: Yes, but this list is updated weekly and includes new companies. The high accuracy rate will save us money on returned mailing pieces.'

'That settee you've ordered – it's a bit bigger than I'd wanted for that corner of the room.'

To partner: 'Yes, I know it's bigger than the other ones we've seen, but it has a high back so it lessens the chance of back pain. Imagine if you had to take time off work for back ache – you've got so much on your plate at the moment.'

We raise certain questions with salespeople to try to get the answers we want. They're not objections – just additional facts to help us decide and perhaps 'sell' our purchase to somebody with a vested interest who might raise real objections.

So the hard and fast rule is: *differentiate* between true objections and demands for *reassurance*. Good psychology can help us look into the real reasons for various objections – and also recognize those that are just 'excuses' from the buyer to try to terminate the meeting. Few people feel comfortable in saying 'no' to a proposition. So they'll pick up on point after point that will enable them to wriggle out of the proposition, with the minimum of discomfort.

Top of the list of common objections is *price*. The majority of price objections are not what they seem. Get inside the mind; don't get on the defensive. What the other person is often really saying is this: OK, your price is higher than your competitors, I'm feeling insecure about the possibility of being ripped off. I don't want to look a fool at the end of the day. So tell me *what* it is that makes people buy your product at such a high price. If it makes sense, I'm willing to pay it.

So you hit him with the reasons. And if you can convince him of your unique selling proposition (USP) then stage two begins.

The buyer may now want to find out if objecting to your price can yield a discount or some other concession. If your mind reading has been effective earlier, you may have picked up on some facets that are important to him. For example, he may have a cash flow problem or storage limitations. So you may be able to offer something other than a price discount that could be even more valuable to him.

Most purchasers have an in-built fear that somebody else may be getting the same product from you at a lower price. So their attitude is: if you don't ask, you don't get. But they don't necessarily have to win more from you in monetary terms.

We should remember that generally people don't buy on price. They buy on quality or *value*. It's very unwise to start a sales meeting on price, just because the prospect has asked right from the start 'How much?' before giving you the opportunity to establish value. He may dwell on the price angle and so be distracted for the duration of the meeting, missing most of your points relating to value.

Fact: a lot of purchases are made just on the strength of the personality and knowledge of the salesperson. *You* are included under 'value'. You are very much part of the package. Selling is firstly about selling yourself. You are part of that product you are selling. You're unique in your own way. Other companies selling a similar product don't have you. Remember: *There will always be competitors, but the one thing that they haven't got is You.*

Many prospects will have done their homework with regard to your rivals and will therefore be well armed to fire objections. Often they will have gone through the same exercise with other people. So you'll be tested on your comparative skill at returning the shots.

But is it possible to avoid this battle of wits in the first place? Yes. Skilled negotiators in all walks of life and top salespeople use a very effective psychological technique which works time and time again. The art lies in covering the objection(s) in your presentation so that you've either anticipated or *eliminated* them.

What does that mean exactly? Well, first analyse what an objection is. It's a *negative thought*. Now if a negative thought in the prospect's mind is allowed to come to the surface, it gains greater prominence. Far better if it were left lying, basking in the subconscious waiting for elimination.

If your facts are presented clearly and convincingly and you've covered potential objections in passing, then what seemed like objections in the buyer's mind just disappear. You will come across as a mind reader (just what you're supposed to be!), extremely knowledgeable and in tune with his needs. You've referred to a potential objection that the prospect might have thought too silly to raise, so now he doesn't have to bring it up; that puts less strain on him. He's secretly glad about that. You've made things easy for him now. Selling should be all about making things easy for the other person.

You should remember that there are always some objections that are never ever voiced; they just remain in the buyer's mind, blocking the chance of a sale. If you can demolish them based on what you found out using your ESP (empathy, sincerity, perspicacity) techniques, you're in a very favourable position.

If you can become master of all the likely objections that could come up about your product, through previous experiences, you will be equipped to bring them into your presentation naturally – before the prospect voices any of them. You cover the points in a matter-of-fact way. The presentation then runs smoothly with the minimum of negative interruptions.

There is one point which salespeople generally tend to overlook. Many people raise a particular objection because they are confused about an aspect that has been touched upon. It hasn't been explained clearly and they've got the wrong end of the stick. But if they are really confused and just don't understand, they might not bother to ask for it to be clarified. (Nobody wants to look like an idiot.) So they'll just put the salesman off with an artificial objection – even if they're *interested* in his overall proposition. So he loses a possible sale because he didn't read the other person's reactions to a weak spot in his presentation.

Always check whether you're making yourself clear by observing facial expressions, sensing hesitation and other giveaway signs. You can almost see a slowing down of the 'tape drive' in somebody's head when it receives a message that can't be decoded. That person might look dubious or puzzled, for instance. You can't afford to miss the signs. Back to ESP again.

So watch and listen carefully!

5

Holding attention

If you want to keep the attention of an audience, whether it be one or two people or a hundred, you must keep them interested.

But it's very difficult to keep the interest level constant. Attention is held only when interest is rising. We spoke about the problem of the mind being able to engage in competing thoughts while seemingly paying attention to something else. Sure, we're listening – but not 'hearing'. Most people assume the two actions are complementary. But they're not – as this overheard conversation illustrates:

'So what did you do at the weekend then?'

'Drove down to the coast with the kids, to Brighton, and stayed overnight.'

'Oh Brighton. I haven't been there for years. Did you take the train?'

'No, I drove there.'

'Did you go on your own?'

Zzzzzzzzzzzzzzzzzzzzzzzzzzzz! Disastrous. The questioner edited the conversation until he found a key word that sparked his interest – and then of course he'd missed all the other details. They were just words which he had chosen not to register.

People fool themselves into thinking that they're good listeners; they're probably good hearers. But that doesn't allow them to take interest in, and thus make use of, what they are told to further business and/or social relationships. The wife says to her husband, who's sitting in an armchair looking at the television:

'You will mow the lawn for me tomorrow, won't you?'

'What? Oh yes, yes.'

'We've got to get to the theatre by six, so we ought to leave now.'

'Yes. OK, OK.'

'I was going to wear this dress – but do you think it makes my bottom look big?'

'Yes, yes.'

'What? You think it's big?'

'What? No – I mean no.'

'You just said "yes" to everything. It shows that you never listen to anything I say.'

Ouch! What could make the situation even worse is that although this man was looking at the television, he was probably only hearing and not listening to the sound. And he wasn't listening to his wife. He was listening to his *own* thoughts in his own head.

For our part, how can we encourage people to listen to us? By keeping them interested in what we have to say, so that they won't get bored and start listening to *themselves*.

Actors on stage know very well that their success depends on maintaining audience attention. Their aim is to make interest rise for the maximum length of time and try to prevent it falling. They're having to compete with the audience's mental and visual distractions. A lapse of attention by a member of the audience during a 'boring' scene will let in all sorts of extraneous thoughts:

'Mmm. I hope the car will be all right parked where it is. It was sticking out from the corner a bit. If Sue's aunt hadn't phoned we wouldn't have been late – then we could have got into the car park. Still, it's now a lot nearer than the car park. I hope I can find it later. Oh yes, I know. It's near that pizza place. They do nice pizzas there. Maybe we'll eat there later. Now, have I got my cheque book? No, Sue's got it in her handbag. What's that thing on the edge of the stage? Oh, it's a revolver. I wonder if she knows she's got a ladder in her stocking . . .'

By the time he tries to get back into the swing of the play he finds that he's lost interest and it's hard to regain it.

The same problem exists in everyday business situations. How do you stop the buyer from switching off while you are having your say?

Take a typical meeting situation where the salesperson is visiting the prospective client's office (note: this could equally be an employee and his boss, a job interview, or in fact any kind of 'meeting'):

You enter the client's office and take the seat offered. After a few pleasantries you begin your presentation.

Three minutes into your spiel, his telephone rings. 'Do excuse me for a minute' he says, taking the call. After two or three minutes, when he has finished: 'Now. Where were we? I'm sorry. Please carry on.'

You recall where you left off and continue talking. He nods as you are speaking and you feel that he's with you.

About two minutes later his secretary walks in. 'Excuse me' she says to both of you, and then to her boss 'Would you sign this please. It's very urgent.' He apologises to you and stares at a cheque. He questions his secretary about a certain point relating to the amount. He then asks her to locate some paperwork from the files. She leaves.

You pick up your thread and afterwards ask the client some questions. He's speaking now.

Five minutes on, the secretary returns with some documents. Apologies again, as he studies various invoices. He seems disturbed by something; pensively he picks up his pen, signs the cheque and hands it over. She leaves the room.

You now realize that there is a breakdown of attention here. He's definitely not with it now. You're wasting your breath. You can barely remember what you've said; what hope for him? However, you carry on.

A woman enters with two cups of coffee.

Half-way through your preamble on price, his phone rings. More apologies. It's his boss wanting some figures for the departmental meeting in twenty minutes time. He puts the phone down and starts fumbling through his in-tray. 'Do carry on talking' he says to you, as he flicks through sheets of paper searching for the required report. He doesn't find it. He looks defeated. 'I'm sorry. One of those days. Keep talking. But could I ask you to be brief?' Brief?

This is a tragic scenario – but quite a common one. Most of us have experienced it (or subjected somebody to something similar). The point: *it's difficult to control attention when there isn't any in the first place*. The example highlights what happens in varying degrees in many meetings and interviews. There is a breakdown of attention which is totally beyond our control.

It would be better, at the point of being asked to be brief, for you the salesman to call a halt to the proceedings. You could suggest returning another time – when the client is less likely to be distracted and/or under time pressure.

To continue under such unfavourable circumstances would be a waste of time and effort; the other person's mind is elsewhere. A hurried discussion is fair to neither party. Try the suggestion of making another appointment. The inconvenience involved may not seem worth while, but if the prospect agrees to see you again he may well have some feeling of guilt which could work in your favour. He's messed you around and you've then helped him out of a tight spot. The next time you should at least be heard in a more sympathetic vein.

This sort of indebtedness often helps people to get what they actually want from others. It's just human nature at work; if you've upset somebody's plans then you will usually go out of your way to compensate somehow. This is not, of course, the ideal way for two people to do business or conduct a relationship. But it happens. Restoring the balance is the most important thing.

Keeping the audience's attention or interest is probably the bedrock of successful selling. Everything else follows from that. No attention – means no communication – means no result. But most salespeople fail to *recognize* when somebody's attention is wavering. It's up to you to pick up the signals and act accordingly.

The problem is this. When presenting a sales pitch, an idea or a demand, it's usually crucial to get the point across at the first attempt — assuming conditions are conducive. This initial discussion shapes the eventual outcome. Having rejected an idea in the first instance, most people do not like to change their minds later — even if they know they're wrong. It's a question of pride. They don't want to look indecisive or incapable of making the right evaluation in the first place.

Who wants to waste a sales pitch on somebody whose mind is simply not there? If your proposal is only half heard then your chances of success are reduced by 50 per cent immediately. So if you want somebody to buy your product, to agree to your demand for a new office desk, to accept your proposal of marriage or your reasons for handing in your resignation, then you need their full attention. Otherwise try to defer the conversation. Remember: you usually only get one chance.

The numerous interruptions experienced in the situation just described can be analysed to show the possible effect on the client's *receptiveness*: in other words, how the disturbances affect his attention span.

1   In the first three minutes he has absorbed most of what you, the salesperson, have said.
2   Telephone rings. His mind is now on the subject of the telephone conversation (the advertising agency wants to know whether to amend the copy for the new advertisement: could he call them back by 3 p.m.?) He puts the phone down.
3   You go on talking and he nods repeatedly (thinking to himself, while 'listening', 'Mmm, maybe we should have spot colour for the logo').
4   His secretary brings the cheque to be signed. He's not satisfied and asks her to return with some supporting documents.
5   You continue talking and the prospect listens (but he's thinking 'How could the cheque be for that much? They must have made an addition error or — I know — I bet

they're trying to sting us for . . .'). You ask him a question relating to the computer software used by his company. But the client isn't prepared – he's on the wrong track because he's missed most of what has been said.

6 Secretary returns with documents. He reluctantly signs the cheque.

7 You begin to talk – but now you can almost see the client's 'wheels' turning ('I should have queried that invoice with the suppliers; their bills never show a meaningful breakdown. The financial director's really going to give me a hard time at the departmental meeting . . .'). But all the time he's nodding away in acknowledgement of what's being said.

How deceptive. But it's up to you to look for the signs. You can tell by the eyes and other expressions whether the mind is elsewhere. If you know you've lost the other person's attention, it's better to stop.

The attention curve

Audience attention is best represented as a curve. Maintaining a steady rise is virtually impossible. The ideal curve would be very hard or impossible for anyone to attain (see Figure 1). The curves are more likely to be formed with intermittent waves; attention would be gained, would fall away and then be built up again (see Figure 2).

Fact: people often lose the thread of a conversation *and* need something explained again. But they won't *admit* it. There are numerous reasons for this:

1 *They don't want to seem impolite.*
2 *They don't want to look stupid.*
3 *They feel guilty for letting their minds wander.*
4 *They don't want to prolong the meeting because they have another engagement lined up; or they've just got a lot to do.*

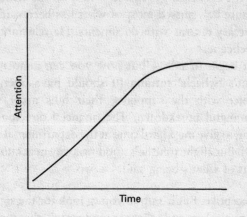

Figure 1   *Ideal attention curve: attention is held and maintained right from the start*

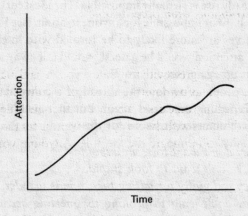

Figure 2   *Typical attention curve, with intermittent waves*

5   *They have decided they're not interested and they 'switch off'.*

If this happens to you in any selling situation, it's your responsibility to take corrective action to regain the person's attention.

Programme your mind to retain an attention curve – to be applied in *any* meeting situation. *This will allow you to visualize the peaks and troughs in your dialogue,* You'll be able to evaluate lapses of concentration that much better. When you see it happening, you should try to find out why. Are you being boring? Or have they missed a main point? Or were you speaking in jargon? Because we can't see the other's mind 'two-timing' us we have to look for the giveaway signals, or be alert and understanding enough to notice when concentration lapses.

You should be aware of the different types of distractions that can cause loss of concentration:

1   *Client disagrees with something you've said (and starts thinking about it).*
2   *Visual distractions.*
3   *Interruptions from other people.*

Client disagrees

A client who disagrees with something you've said may go off at a tangent in his own mind and so lose the thread of what you're saying. In some cases, if you've said something that he strongly disagrees with, he may just be waiting for the earliest opportunity to terminate the meeting. Anything you say is wasted.

Visual distractions

A visual distraction is anything that triggers our overactive minds, forcing us to blot out the message coming across to us.

Such distractions are all around:

1   If you're watching *Hamlet* on stage and Ophelia is wearing a watch, then the distraction is so great that you probably miss the dialogue and artistry.
2   You're with a client in a restaurant and he suddenly spots somebody he knows seated in the far corner. He constantly looks away to see if that person has noticed him; you can see his attention wavering.
3   If you're talking to somebody who has a stain on their jacket, or a prominent button missing with the loose thread hanging, that can be enough to distract your mind from following the gist of the conversation. The flaw in the person's appearance fills your mind.

If you rip your sleeve on the reception filing cabinet coming in, or you lose a vital button in the car park – and you know this – then tell the other person. His knowing that *you* know should then be enough to stop his mind wondering about the offending flaw. Case closed.

If there's to be a meeting in your office and there are potential visual distractions there, try to anticipate. Turn the Pirelli calendar the other way round!

Constant interruptions

It's unproductive if your presentation is continually disturbed when you're with a client on his home ground. The attention curve for the earlier example is shown in Figure 3.

But as the working environment becomes increasingly pressurized, this situation is now more or less a certainty. As the new breed of workaholic multiplies, with people taking on more and more, few meetings between salesperson and prospect are completely free of interruption. You have to live with it. Inevitably the onus is on the prospector to carry out the salvage operation.

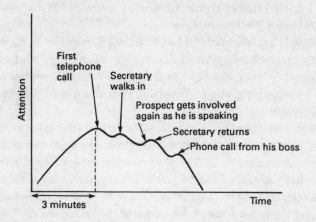

Figure 3   *Attention curve showing interruptions and their effect*

If the disruption is in human form you can at least categorize the nature of any problem involved because you hear what is said. You can then evaluate its possible effect on your listener's concentration. With a telephone distraction, you have to try to observe the prospect's facial expressions and check the tone of voice if the conversation is monosyllabic. It could be:

1 His boss giving him a dressing down.
2 His wife announcing she's leaving him.
3 Production department telling him that delivery for a major client won't go out on time.
4 An irate client threatening to cancel a sizeable contract.
5 His secretary informing him his car's been clamped.

Unless he refers to the phone call, you'll have to guess from the eyes and tone as to his likely level of distraction. If he looks mildly or seriously preoccupied, then what is the answer?

Repeat. I repeat: repeat. Give him a summary of what you said before the interruption.

People are always afraid of sounding parrot-like in their presentations. But consider this: *people only take in about 40 per cent of what they hear.* And that's *without* interruptions. So by recapping, you're increasing your chances of making your point stick.

After an interruption, visualize the mental attention curve and pick up on the points made before you were silenced. You can do this briefly. His new problem has blotted out part of what you said earlier, so you're helping him to come back into the discussion. You're into his mind and working out where the breakdowns have occurred. So rescue the discussion – and save the situation.

By summarizing what you've said, each time, you're also helping him to crystallize in his own mind all the benefits that you've been selling. By being able to extract the salient points of your pitch, you're showing that your line of thinking is logical and structured. It enhances your stature.

It's impossible to get totally undivided attention as long as the listener is capable of stray thoughts. It does help, though, to recognize how supplementary thoughts caused by interruptions can defocus your own presentation. If we know how to recognize it, we can at least do something about it.

Ways to win more attention

Don't be desk-bound

The scene of most selling situations is the prospective client's office. The desk separates buyer and seller. The problem is that the buyer cannot get away (mentally or physically) from the piled-up proof on his desk of all the work awaiting him.

So what? Anybody conducting a meeting from behind

their desk is bound to be all too aware of the paperwork waiting there to be done. You know from your own experience: it's there in front of you, reminding you of how busy you are. (*In fact, I'm so busy, what the hell am I doing talking to this person?*) This allows all sorts of random thoughts to enter the head: 'Mmm. I must remember to write a reply to that letter. Oh, the productivity memo. I must get that out by Friday – oh no, my secretary has spelt "analysis" wrong . . .'

It's a consequence of being on your own territory. You can see your own workload seeming to grow in front of your eyes, bringing distraction with it. A vague anxiety sets in. It's not fair on the salesperson. The meeting was agreed. But the prospect isn't hearing a thing. It's showing on his face – an impatience to start tackling his workload.

The salesman should be aware of this territorial problem. He can thus try to avoid it if at all possible. If you've experienced the desk-bound type before, you would be wise to try to get him out of the hot seat to a calmer corner of the room: in other words, away from his desk. If it's obvious that the setting for your presentation is unfavourable to you, then take the lead in changing the scene. You can perhaps innocently put your belongings down on an alternative table or chair. This often encourages the other person to move away from his desk and use this new area for your meeting.

Magic wand principle

Just as a magician's wand is used to control and divert audience attention (in the interests of his art), so the use of a pen as a pointer can work wonders. It helps the other person to focus on your brochures, printouts or whatever. It helps blot out other visual distractions. If you are using *his* pen, so much the better. He won't be able to keep his eyes off it.

There's an interesting phenomenon about people and pens – together. If somebody lends you a pen, even for a brief moment, they always assume you're going to walk off with it!! They'll watch you intently until they've got their possession back. It really makes people pay attention to what you're doing with it.

When you use a pen to indicate something, you're giving the other person a point of focus. Of course you should be equipped with your own pen; but if you do find yourself with somebody whose concentration seems to be slipping, then ask if you can borrow his.

Using the person's name (for attention)

There's nothing that 'snaps you out of it' quite like the sound of your name heard through a blitz of competing sounds — those inside your own head, and extraneous noises such as other people speaking or general office bustle.

Like other animals, we learn from childhood to respond to our own name. When spoken by relative strangers, the sound of one's name is that much more arresting because you don't necessarily expect them to use it. Our name is our most personal possession. Fame is associated with being a 'name'. Everybody would like to be well known.

If using somebody's name brings him to attention, then it can be a useful ploy during a meeting when you sense your listener's mind is wandering. It also works with somebody who gets too buried in the literature you have given him. You know the situation: you've wanted to point out a certain section for him to focus on, but he continues to read the whole thing and not just the part you wanted to highlight. He's probably too engrossed to hear you trying to put him right. Try the name trick to get him to look up straight away: 'So, the point I'm trying to make, Mr Goodwood.' Your presentation doesn't then just sound like a routine exercise, but appears to be a more personal conversation with the client.

You see politicians and interviewers use each other's names all the time to get attention, or to allow them to cut in and score extra points of their own:

'Yes, but Mrs Thatcher, that's not the question I asked you . . .'

'No, no, Terry. You know that it's . . .'

'Now let me finish, Mr Frost.'

Sprinkling a person's name throughout a conversation should be a perfectly natural and respectful gesture. But most people hardly do it at all. It encourages better communication and creates rapport. These are ample reasons for making sure you hear a person's name (as we discuss in Chapter 6) and that you remember it.

Avoid breaks

Awareness of the attention curve reminds you that the best possible situation is to sustain attention on that upward curve as far as you can. Given that most things are bought on an emotional basis (product, idea or whatever), it follows that *timing* is all-important to catch the fleeting emotion that says: 'Yes, I'll have it' or 'Tell me more' or 'OK, you can have that day off.' Anything that lowers that momentary emotional high can turn the decision the other way.

So it's up to you to keep your prospect's attention on that incline and not to *break the spell*.

Imagine you've been watching a film on TV for the last 45 minutes. The car is now 12 feet from the edge of the cliff and the handbrake cable snaps; it's rolling down towards the edge. Click, click: commercial break. When the film resumes after three minutes, do you still have the same feeling? That feeling of sustained drama that had you concentrating intently for three-quarters of an hour? The suspension of disbelief that had completely engrossed you and stopped your own mind wandering for the duration of the film? The short answer to these questions is 'No.' The break has forced you to lose that state of high emotion. The spell's broken.

It's no different in business situations. For example:

A salesman has been talking to the managing director of a hotel group for half an hour. He's been describing a new advanced type of trouser press. The MD is very impressed with the idea of the product and is close to agreeing to purchase some to replace the old models in his bedrooms.

'Have you got the dimensions?' he asks.

'Yes, I'll have those somewhere in my case.'

The salesman picks up his case, opens it and starts to rummage around. As it's taking such a long time, the client turns to some memos on his desk. He has the courtesy to look up a minute later. But as the salesman is still searching frantically, he carries on reading.

'Ah, this is it – no that's . . . wait, I think this is the right one. No I'm sorry. I've got it somewhere here.'

Of course eye contact has been lost now for some time. If the client was having a cardiac arrest, the salesman wouldn't know. He's too busy on a paper chase. The client's emotional state has shifted slightly now. His buying or acceptance level is starting to slip as well as his confidence in the salesman. His thoughts, which had been totally devoted to the trouser press, are now turning to letters he has to sign, what to do for lunch, and why he *shouldn't* buy.

Eventually the salesman locates the sheet of paper. 'Let me see now. There are three sizes actually. All different prices.'

Out comes the calculator: more lost eye contact. 'Well – that doesn't seem right. Maybe I pressed the minus instead of . . . No I couldn't – I think the battery . . .'

Two to three minutes of calculator malfunction follow. Nothing is so boring as watching people tap away at calculator keys. Especially when you don't have confidence in their dexterity. Even worse when you come across those who press 3×4 and then eagerly await the result.

By now our bored managing director has lost that high and has all but come down to earth with a bump. He's had time to think about the product while watching the clumsy antics of the case and calculator double act. This is not an unusual situation; it happens all the time.

It's important to analyse the situation. It's not that the prospect doesn't value the product any more. He is still impressed. It's just that the *feeling* of wanting to buy has gone. He's decided to hang on to his existing trouser presses for a bit longer. They're in good condition. He'll reconsider perhaps next year. He'll go for the same type of product he's just been 'sold', but may well approach another company.

The lesson? If you recognize that most things are bought on an emotional level, then it is important to *get acceptance when feeling is running high*. So avoid having to interrupt your presentation by taking your eyes away from the buyer. If you do that, you're giving him licence to 'stray'. Have your props at hand. If you need to use a calculator – do it slickly. Don't play lucky numbers accompanied by a mumbling commentary.

If you're giving a unit price, let the other person do the calculations. Most people like to work out their own costings. Psychologically, it makes them feel in control. The figure seems more authentic and accurate coming from their own calculations. It helps them to make a decision with more confidence.

The attention curve for this example would look something like Figure 4.

Say what you're going to say . . .

We can perhaps call this the golden rule for effective presentation and holding attention:

Say what you're going to say.
Say it.
Say what you said.

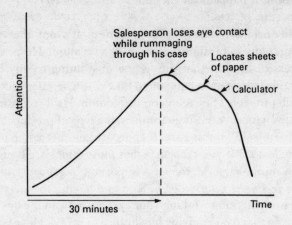

Figure 4   *Example attention curve. For thirty minutes there is good attention, leading to a possible sale; then attention falls sharply*

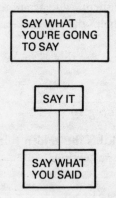

Figure 5   *The golden rule for holding attention*

Firstly, you're telling your audience what you will be speaking about. If it's a subject of interest (and of course you would make sure it was) it keeps people interested. Then you actually tell them about it. Finally, you recap on what you've actually said. On the basis that most people only take in 40 per cent of what they hear, we're using a formula here that increases our chances of being heard.

This principle is also the key to effective letter writing – especially for letters that are intended to sell.

6

Make your memory pay

As a person in business, having to sell yourself, there are huge rewards to be reaped from having a good memory – or developing one.

The problem: a lot of people have very average memories, and many others have very bad ones. If you can break from this mould, you're in a very powerful position.

A poor memory threatens everything in life – health, relationships, income, business contacts. There is just no substitute for a good memory. Most of what we say is founded upon something that has happened, something that we did or that somebody else did. So – if your recall of your own valuable experiences, or others' words of wisdom is that bit better than the average person's, you've got to come out on top.

Remembering names

Remembering names appears to be by far the biggest problem for most business people. And yet the name is the most important piece of information that we need to know about an individual. If you forget somebody's name you're aiming a knockdown shot at the ego – and it's bull's-eye. Although it might not be made obvious, you've lost a few points immediately. Your *faux pas* may only register in the other person's subconscious, but it is still significant.

In many cases it's not that you actually forget a name. *You probably never picked it up in the first place*, because you failed to *hear* it properly and did nothing to rectify this. This could be because:

1 It is an *interest* problem; you just weren't interested enough to fully catch the person's name and 'store' it. Or:
2 You were distracted at the time of the introduction because your mind was elsewhere.

Whatever the reason – it's not good enough. Remembering names is such a potent selling or persuasion tool that, if you do nothing else, you must make the effort to improve in this area.

It seems that when we meet people for the first time, the momentary shock to the system diverts us from our normal listening process. We're so aware of what we look like, what we're going to say and the impression we are giving, that we actually miss the name when it's announced. So it's not that we've forgotten the name a few seconds later. It's more likely that we just didn't hear it. But the other person doesn't always know that!

If you don't catch somebody's name at the outset (or if it simply isn't given), the few seconds of handshake afford ample opportunity to ask the other person to repeat it. There is a general reluctance, almost embarrassment about doing this. On the contrary, it demonstrates politeness. A name is the most personal thing we possess; it's unique to us. Consequently, people will be responsive to those who use it.

When you refer to somebody by name, you find that you receive more attention; it's human nature. Whatever 'two-timing', in terms of straying thoughts, may be going on in our head, at the mention of our name our ears prick up.

If you look at the retail sector of selling, the widespread use of credit cards and cheques has led to organizations taking advantage of adding the personal touch by referring to people by name. You see it in banks, restaurants, hotels, at airline check-in desks:

'How would you like your money, Mr . . . ?'

'Enjoy your meal, Miss . . .'

'I hope the room's to your satisfaction, Mr . . .'

'Have a good flight, Mrs . . .'

They've realized the success of such an appeal to vanity. It's a caressing of the ego that works wonders. It's just a simple gesture – but it can have a great effect. Because people like to be known. They go back to places where people know them.

Canny people in any business make a point of committing people's names to memory, whether it be their own or that of a computer – or often both.

It's a fact that, because most products and services face fierce competition, unless you're selling the secret of eternal life you're likely to be in the position of having to sell yourself as well as the product.

There is no better way of selling yourself to someone than being interested enough to remember his name. Sales have been clinched or lost because a person's name was remembered or forgotten. You can improve yourself mentally, just as you can improve your physique from workouts in the gym. Everyone has the ability. Conditioning the mind through mental jogging can help develop a more effective memory for names.

Often, it's not a case of forgetting a name. It's rather that it simply didn't register in the first place. This is simply nothing more than laziness or disinterest. Or nerves. Nerves? Why nerves?

Two people are introduced to each other by a third party. They shake hands. 'Hello – I'm Tim Wilks.' 'Pleased to meet you – John Lett.' It sounds straightforward, but one or the other or both of these people are capable of missing the name because of the worry of what to say next. As they are being introduced, their minds are simultaneously working on the next sentence. The name can be blotted out (refer to Chapter 4). It's not a memory problem in this case; it's a hearing problem.

Think back to some of the parties that you've been to. When you first arrive you are confronted with a room full of faces. You're introduced to a string of people. One by one, names are reeled off: 'John – this is Simon, Glenda, Barbara, Tom, Eileen, Richard . . .' At the same time you are trying to take in many other aspects of the scene – the decor, the people in the background, how much wine there is left, and anything else that catches your eye.

These distractions, combined with your own self-consciousness at meeting all these new people, mean that you probably catch only one or two names, if that. And even then, you don't always attach the right name to the right face. It's not so bad for the people you're being introduced to. They have only *one* name to remember at the time – yours. Also, they have established their territory already – so they're more relaxed. It's much easier to remember things when you're relaxed.

You probably end up gravitating initially towards the two people whose names you happened to catch. *Just your luck – the two biggest bores (those awful types who have taken out their own appendix or done their own conveyancing!).*

Rule 1: *make sure that you hear the name.*

Imagine the following situation, which we may define as a group meeting:

You arrive at the client's office for a meeting with him and three other members of his division – including his boss, the sales director.

As you enter the boardroom, your contact Mr Good introduces you to his three colleagues: 'Nice to see you again. I'd like to introduce you to Edward Fox, our sales director, Douglas Cross from publicity, and Annette Barnes from data processing.'

You fail to hear Mr Fox's name at all. As you shift your case uneasily from your right hand to your left, in readiness to shake his hand, you mutter: 'Er . . . how d'you do.' You manage to catch the names Cross and Barnes: 'How do you do, Mr Cross . . . Miss Barnes.'

You sit down and the discussion starts. Mr Good had mentioned on a previous occasion that his boss, Edward Fox, was the decision maker. Nothing could be agreed, he'd said, unless his boss went along with it. But his boss was apparently a reasonable man – a 'people' person – who liked to know he was dealing with somebody he could trust. Hence the group meeting in which he wanted to be present.

Since you can't remember this man's name, you find yourself addressing Mr Cross, whose name you caught, and also your original contact Mr Good. (Your subconscious registered the name Cross because it's also the name of the street where you live.) Mr Cross happens to be the least influential member of the group as far as this project is concerned. Yet you end up directing most of your points at him. Why? Because you know his name and can refer to it in the conversation.

The others, Mr Fox and Miss Barnes, are not given as much attention. Yet they are the two people with the power to agree to the proposal. It is with them that you should have been trying hard to establish some kind of rapport.

This scenario occurs every day in business meetings (and socially). It does not promote effective communication. But it's so easy to avoid. And what positive results are achieved by doing so!

It's so simple. At the start, the obvious statement 'I'm sorry, I didn't catch the name' would have been the solution. But people don't do it. Why?

People seem to assume that the attitude of the other person is: 'Either you get my name the first time – or forget it!' As though it's an unforgiveable *faux pas*. As though the person who has dared to ask for the name to be repeated should be written off as slow, stupid, unprofessional or all three.

Don't ever feel embarrassed about admitting that you didn't hear a name. There's a twin advantage:

1 You are actually sure of the name.
2 As a psychological plus, you make the person you are meeting feel *more important*. You've shown that you consider it worth knowing his or her name.

Rule 2: *if you hear a name, make sure you put it to the right face*.

If you have ever got people's names crossed during a meeting, it's probably something you never want to do again. The embarrassment is so great that if you are ever in any doubt you will probably end up using no names at all. And this will definitely reduce your effectiveness as a communicator whose aim is to create rapport with a particular set of individuals. Certainly, calling the person by the wrong name is infinitely worse than not remembering the name at all.

A useful tip for matching names to faces of people at a group meeting is to take first letters of names and line them up in your mind (according to the seating) to form a word or abbreviation. The dictionary name for this is 'mnemonics'.

Take for example the names of the people at the meeting just mentioned: Mr Cross, Mr Fox and Miss Barnes. Assuming they are safely seated so you know where they are, you can repeat C-B-F, C-B-F in your head a few times to ensure that you know exactly who is who. Try it the next time you're in this kind of situation; it's a simple but effective aid.

If you want to test how much importance you subconsciously attach to names, catch yourself when you're at a business conference, seminar or other function. Delegates are probably wearing the obligatory plastic lapel name badges. You spot a familiar face but can't remember the name. That may deter you from actually going up to her and catching up on business news. But if it doesn't, you end up not concentrating on the conversation because you're trying to sneak a look at the name of the lapel badge.

She's remembered your name *and* your company. That's put even more stress on you. You feel terribly embarrassed. You've been so intent on trying to read her name badge – but the light's been shining on the plastic and you couldn't see – that you've missed most of what she's said. She asks you a question related to the discussion. You're at a loss because you haven't been listening. This looks like disinterest. She thinks you're a waste of time and moves off at the earliest opportunity.

You still didn't get her name. And now she's got the wrong impression about you, besides everything else.

Sometimes it pays to ask somebody else, discreetly, the name of the person concerned. 'My memory's going – who's that over there?' If you don't know the person that well, and it's quite in order that it may have slipped your mind (i.e. it wouldn't cause offence), then 'Sorry, your name's escaped me' is permissible. Sometimes (if you're lucky) the person in question, if in a group, will automatically identify himself with a handshake to a new arrival. That solves your problem.

The recognition factor is a strong streak running through all of us. To be recognized is a measure of esteem, an inner satisfaction. People know me. The ego's hunger for recognition provides another area of opportunity to gain points. Your name is the label of recognition.

The direct marketing industry has grown up around the success of dealing directly with named people. More and more organizations are discovering the benefits of marketing their products directly to a person once they have their name and address. Both consumer and business-to-business direct mail have shown staggering growth in recent years. The name is a powerful tool.

The cashless society has presented an instant opportunity for being personal. 'Thank you very much Miss Banks, I hope you enjoy the book' as you're handed back your cheque card. Your first experience of after-sales service – seconds after the sale! The lingering impression of the bookstore is one of warmth.

A *true story*

A sales manager is going to the United States for a meeting with prospective clients, arranged by the local advertising agency executive over there.

When he arrives in the US, the sales manager, Thomas Hart, telephones the agency man, Chuck Madsen, to find out the arrangements for the meeting. His call is greeted by an answerphone. He leaves this message: 'Hello Chuck. It's Thomas Hart from London. I'm in San Francisco now and I'm at Hotel . . .'

The next day he has a call from Chuck: 'Tom. It's Chuck Madsen here. Good to talk to you . . . Meeting's fixed for tomorrow at 10.30. I'll pick you up about 10 o'clock.'

The following day they meet as arranged and proceed to the client's offices. On their arrival, two men greet them. Chuck says: 'Bill, Pete, I'd like to introduce you to our friend from London – Thomas Clarke.'

What should Tom do now? Does he say 'Actually it's Tom H-a-r-t' and embarrass Chuck?

'Good to meet you, Mr Clarke. Hope you didn't bring any fog over from London. We've enough of our own.' They both shake hands with him. 'Hey, can we call you Tom?' ('Please – anything but Clarke' he thinks.)

Tom's performance during the interview is completely stilted. Naturally enough he doesn't feel comfortable with his new-found identity. Of course he is eventually given a business card by each of the new acquaintances. He automatically feels for his own, but quickly retracts. This is now completely out of the question.

He blames Chuck. He accepts the difficulties of hearing a name over the phone, long distance, but Chuck should have double checked it at the start. His unease is now total – like a criminal on the run adopting an alias. All his effort is now spent trying to save face and avoiding embarrassing the others. He can't concentrate and so is unable to give his best performance.

Subconsciously, he's now dreading an order from the clients. He doesn't want a sale, because the *faux pas* would then be revealed. He regrets not correcting the name at the outset – but then Chuck would have lost face.

After the uninspired meeting, Tom leaves with Chuck. He considers telling him about the problem. But he doesn't want to make him feel a fool, even now. With any luck, there will be no sale thanks to his unimpressive presentation. So he probably won't see these people again. Fortunately, he receives no calls at the hotel over the next two days. He leaves for London.

Two years later he is speaking to one of his bosses who has just returned from the US west coast.

'I saw a guy called Chuck Madsen last week. Apparently you met him a couple of years ago. Spoke very highly of you – except he was a bit puzzled about something.'

'Oh, what?'

'Said you went around calling yourself C-l-a-r-k-e and not H-a-r-t!'

Well, what went wrong? Perhaps:

1 Chuck simply may not have listened properly; or
2 He may have just forgotten the name; or
3 The telephone was to blame for blurring the message to Chuck Madsen.

In any case, to be absolutely sure, Chuck should have checked with hotel reception, or should have just clarified it from Tom Hart when they first met. Perfectly in order in such circumstances.

Instead, all parties lost out:

1 Chuck could have enhanced his reputation by introducing his clients to somebody with the means of making their campaigns more successful. He would have had some reflected glory, and it would have strengthened the bond between advertising agency and client.
2 The clients lost out on a UK connection that would have benefited them.

3   Tom Hart missed out on a lucrative and prestigious sale
    for which he had spent a lot of time preparing. And he felt
    embarrassed about contacting Chuck Madsen again. He
    had even left the country without calling to say goodbye.
    Not at all the sort of impression he really wanted to
    create.

It could be argued that it was partly Tom's fault. When he
first met Chuck he could have introduced himself again just
to make sure. Or he should, as a matter of courtesy, have
handed over his business card at the start. That would have
nullified any embarrassment within Madsen's mind, because
up till then he wouldn't have actually mentioned Hart's
name.

Business cards can be trumps

If we acknowledge the importance of a name in establishing good business relations, then it follows that if somebody
gets it wrong the embarrassment can be fatal to the relationship. The perpetrator of the mistake may well feel unable to
face the victim again. Now that's not good for either
party.

The business card is now universal ('Could I have your
card?', 'Here's my card'), yet there are some people who take
great delight in not having them precisely because of their
being in such common use. But there's no question that a card
is useful for four reasons:

1   It establishes the image of your company.
2   It provides your name and *status* immediately.
3   You have it in front of you in case you forget the person's
    name in the course of the conversation.
4   It can provide an interesting opener to the meeting, and
    establishes initial ice-breaking conversation (remember
    the 'first six minutes' in Chapter 3).

People vary in their preference as to when they hand over their cards. Offering yours at the *beginning* of a meeting generally helps the client to remember your name and to evaluate your status. He will usually reciprocate, allowing you to confirm or evaluate *his* position too. But some clients hand over their card at the end of a meeting.

If you think you'll have trouble remembering the person's name or are unsure of it, then be sure to exchange cards at the start when you arrive. Then keep his in view so that you can refer to it. He's probably doing the same with yours. It's on his desk in front of him. He doesn't want to get your name wrong either.

The following is a true story. A businessman on holiday in the South of France was sunbathing by the hotel swimming pool. He struck up a conversation with a Japanese executive who was swimming up and down the length of the pool. After a few minutes of discussion the swimmer made his way to the edge of the pool where his partner in conversation was seated. He then put his right hand down the front of his swimming trunks and to the surprise – and delight – of the onlookers, produced a *waterproof* business card which he handed to the other man.

Importance of a good memory in business

The vast majority of people have average memories. So if yours is *acute*, you really stand out. You conjure up facts, figures and names out of thin air and use them to your advantage in the selling process. Remember: Filofaxes can't store everything – and they can get lost!

If you remember something about a person, he feels flattered; you're appealing to his ego.

'You went to Sardinia two months ago. How was it?'

'When we spoke in March you'd just exchanged contracts on your house; are you in there yet?'

'You were having problems with the contractors over your
new office, the last time I was here. Sorted out now?'

In a sales situation, remembering things shows the buyer that
you are interested in him and his business and gives you
credibility. You're not just an automaton. You're not just
there to sell. You are an interested human being.

In today's selling environment, it is not enough just to be
geared up about your product. People are looking for more
than that. They want you to be knowledgeable about their
particular industry. You're supposed to be helping them.
How can you be of any real help if you don't know much
about *their* business? You need to draw upon a good store of
knowledge in order to cover different client interests and
requirements. That calls for a good memory.

To make way for valuable information to be stored in the
mind, it's necessary to declutter it. You have to relegate
useless information to the back of your mental filing cabinet.
There are people who can give you the FA Cup results since
1964 but can't remember their telephone number. They can
recite the last ten minutes of 'Gone With the Wind' but can't
remember your wife's name. A readjustment is needed.

The first essential is a conscious effort to *be* interested. One
person's lack of knowledge about another results from no
effort being made to take an interest. Even in a friendship,
sometimes sympathy and understanding can be a sadly one-
way affair. Some people are so superficial in their dealings
with others that they can be caught out. For example:

'How's things, Mark?'

'Well – business isn't that good at the moment. And I had a
burglary last week . . .'

Good. I wanted to talk to . . .'

How can you possibly remember things if you don't programme your mind to register what the other person is

saying? It's selfishness really. If you want something from another person – friendship, help, money, sympathy, business – you've got to be interested enough to remember things connected with them. It allows you to establish a productive two-way relationship.

The simplest way to improve memory is by *association*. You may come across people with whom you have something in common; this ought to help you to remember facts about *them*. It could be many things: age, birthplace, love of a sport, car, holiday, name, parrot's birthday. This common factor can easily trigger a memory association. And since the other person's memory isn't that good, he's *forgotten* he ever told you about his new car, his holiday, his recent accident or whatever. As a result, when you say to him:

'How's your Ferrari X3 running?'

'Have you played any hockey recently?'

'What did you do on your birthday last week?'

he can't help but be surprised – and impressed. 'How did you know . . .?'

The following is a true story. A sales executive has the same birthday as a client's daughter. He picked up this information quite by accident. During a late meeting one day the prospect mentioned that he couldn't spare more than an hour as he had to get back for his daughter's birthday party. It was also this salesman's birthday. He mentioned to the prospect that he shared the same birthday as his daughter.

A year later, the two men happened to meet at the same exhibition on exactly the same date. The sales executive said to the man: 'How are you celebrating your daughter's birthday today?'

The man nearly collapsed. He might just have accepted that somebody could have found out *his* birthday – but not his five-year-old daughter's!! Of course he couldn't remember the mutual birthday from the meeting the previous year. That man is now a good client. You see, most people have poor memories.

Empty promises

A particularly disturbing habit prevalent in both business and social situations causes more upsets and misunderstandings than anything else. That is the making of empty promises and statements.

In many cases the person who is promised something that doesn't materialize, forgets anyway – and so no harm is done. Relationships continue and business keeps functioning. But in many instances what turned out to be empty words are forgotten by the speaker – but *remembered by the listener*. In business, particularly in sales, this can be disastrous.

Consider this situation:

Salesman: 'Well – I'll see you when I get back from my jaunt on the other side of the Atlantic.'

'Where are you going exactly?'

'Boston. It's a prize. I won a contest.'

'Oh – congratulations. That's great. All that lovely maple syrup there for the eating. I'm envious.'

'You've been there, have you?'

'Worked there for 5 years – beautiful place.'

'You like maple syrup?'

'Yes. Love it.'

'I'll bring you some back.'

'Hey – that's kind of you, but there's no need to take the trouble.'

'No. It'll be no trouble for you. A pleasure.'

'Well if you're sure. My wife will be pleased. Thanks.'

Typically, the salesman has forgotten this conversation by the time he's got back to the visitors' car park minutes later. The buyer has a good memory. He even tells his wife that evening to expect some maple syrup from Boston, courtesy of a thoughtful new contact.

Three weeks later this 'thoughtful' salesman returns from his travels and makes a follow-up appointment.

Prospect: 'Well. How was Boston?'

The salesman is flattered. He feels important. 'What a nice man' he thinks. 'He remembers I went to Boston. I can't remember telling him about the trip.' Salesman: 'Have you been there?'

'Er . . . why, yes. I was there for 5 years. Don't you remember me saying last time?'

'Oh er er. That's right. Of course.' It's obvious from his face that he doesn't remember. Or that the recollection is very vague.

The disillusioned client is now doubting the integrity of somebody so apparently superficial. He has already almost written him off. During the rest of the presentation there is no mention of the gift that had been promised so effusively.

The buyer had made his final evaluation of the salesman well before escorting him to the lift. He'd decided that the man was *insincere*. (His inner feeling was: if you can forget this, you'll forget to service me adequately after a sale – and you probably also forgot to tell me the drawbacks of your product!!)

The moral is: woe betide you with your broken promises if the other person has a good memory. You'll come unstuck.

Come on: *get inside the mind*. Forgetting a throwaway line – which was quite incidental to your sale – may seem a trivial thing to you. But it may be a significant one to the other person involved. It's important to remember: people have very different levels of *sensitivity*.

Casual remarks or promises, that may seem unimportant to you, may strike a chord with the other person. You're then expected to come up with the goods. If you fail to do so your true worth as a person is in doubt – and it becomes hard to alter that judgement. Like the buyer in the story above, many people would use such behaviour as a barometer of the salesman's integrity.

A poor memory causes friendships to fall apart, marriages to break up, business relationships to fracture. But there's really no excuse. As already established, it's an interest problem; so it can be cured. You're not taking sufficient interest to remember things that are important to people with whom you are dealing.

You must make the effort to pick up people's reactions and sensitivities to what you are saying or doing in any kind of relationship. More often than not the other party will not convey his real feelings about your sin(s) of omission. Your forgetfulness or thoughtlessness is quite likely to result in a rift. You could lose business – or a friend. And you may not even know why.

Take everyday situations. A friend lends you £10 to save you queuing at the bank; you forget to pay her back. Another friend buys your theatre ticket, as you've left your credit card in the car; you forget. Your secretary reminds you about your wife's birthday. You promise to buy your secretary a bottle of bubbly for her thoughtfulness; you forget. Eventually, you find these people have no time for you. And you can't think why. They give you the cold shoulder. And you can't even dig in your memory bank to work out the reason – because it's permanently on overdraft. You never put anything in!!'

Nobody wants the embarrassment of reminding you that you have not paid your debts or fulfilled your promises. You should make a point of remembering in the first place what you commit yourself to.

Make your memory pay.

Memory improving tricks

Remembering figures

Of course in a business context there is a great need to be on

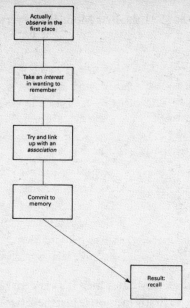

Figure 6   *Steps to attaining a productive memory*

top of figures, to remember dates, prices and technical details. But there really is no problem even for the person with a so-called bad memory. It's just a question of making a *conscious* effort to remember perhaps other figures that *mean something to you* already. The process is shown in Figure 6.

Want proof? I bet you could memorize the calendar for a particular year with no trouble at all. So if somebody walked up to you and said: 'What day of the week is 25 November next year and 29 April the following year?', you wouldn't abuse them and suggest they invest in a good diary. You'd conjure up the figures from thin air in a matter of seconds. Or more accurately – your memory would.

You don't believe it? Have a go. Prove it to yourself.

Like most memory feats, we're first of all looking for *interest*. Be interested enough to commit a few dates to memory. And I don't mean 365 days either. Let's take twelve.

For example, in 1991 the first Monday of every month falls as follows:

January	7
February	4
March	4
April	1
May	6
June	3
July	1
August	5
September	2
October	7
November	4
December	2

If you know these key dates then it's very easy to work out any date at all. So firstly memorize just these twelve digits. It's easy to do this if you pair up, i.e. 74 41 63 15 27 42. It's not difficult (ask any judge in a Miss World contest!). Now repeat these six figures and make a conscious effort to remember. Repeat them out loud nine times. Got it?

Now, suppose you're trying to work out what day 14 November is in 1991. November is the eleventh month, and so the first Monday is the 4th; therefore the 14th is a Thursday. You see, you've done it – in seconds. (For 1992, the corresponding first Monday figures would be 63 26 48 63 75 27.)

The effect on your audience would be astounding. But isn't it easy to make yourself have a good memory? The key is *association*. As established earlier – a good memory is all about association. We associate something *we already know* (and hence remember) to provide us with an answer to something else we *would like to know* (and remember). Just by remembering six figures you have suddenly become, to others, a walking calendar. It's magic. The magic of memory.

Remembering prices

You may need to remember prices, discounts and other figures relating to various products on offer. Of course there is usually a price list that you may be able to refer to, which means that most business people do not take the time or trouble to commit these figures to memory. But what about when you need to think on your feet? Being able to remember prices without recourse to written material can often mean the difference between deal or no deal.

How? Well, it's all tied up with the *attention curve*, which you'll remember from the previous chapter (now there's a memory test for you!). Remember the importance of *timing* in the selling process: how an interruption can disturb that emotional high, that fleeting moment that is make or break. Everything that you've said or done before has been leading up to this *psychological hot spot* of the proceedings. *Successful deals are struck at this point*. You're asked a question about price, discounts or specifications, and your eye contact is suspended as you look away and ponder over written material. The spell is broken – just as when the television commercial appears as the car is heading towards the edge of the cliff.

Now if you were able to memorize prices, for example, you wouldn't have to look away. When the other person says: 'How much will it be for 5000 units, and what discount would you give if I took 14000?' then, instead of breaking the dialogue to rummage through price lists, you answer immediately. You're giving the other person *minimal opportunity to lose concentration* and change emotional state.

Most people do not realize how potent the use of memory is at this sensitive stage. Don't break the dialogue. Come out with the figures naturally and maintain that eye contact. The attention curves for the two situations illustrate how efficient use of memory can change the level of the proceedings (Figure 7).

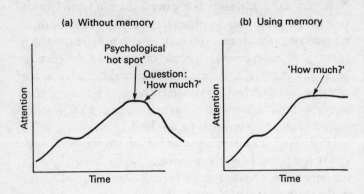

Figure 7   *Maintaining attention by using memory at a crucial moment*

So – what tips can be used to remember prices? Well, it's your *imagination* that provides the key. It will be different for everybody. But firstly – as always – make a conscious decision to memorize and then look for an *association* that you can identify with.

Suppose a pricing structure is as follows:

up to 10 000 units	£1.68 per unit
10 001 to 15 000	£1.42 per unit
15 001 to 20 000	£1.16 per unit
20 001 to 50 000	£0.80 per unit
50 001 plus	£0.34 per unit

Now there's no reason at all for anybody not to be able to have this stored in their memory bank. It's only *laziness*: nothing more, nothing less.

Look how straightforward this structure is. The price per unit drops by a flat 26p up to the third band of 20 000. The bands themselves are in ranges of 5000 up to this figure. Thereafter the drop in rate is 36p and 46p respectively. The final bands are with a range of 30 000, and over 50 000.

If we remember the basic price of 168p, then the rest is easy. We know the reductions after 10 000 are by 26p within the two ranges of 5000. So far so good? And then by 36p and 46p, with the final band being for over 50 000.

So remember the figure 168. See if you can associate it with something you already know. If you're lucky it may be your house number; the first or last three digits of your American Express card; the age of your tortoise. Anything. It doesn't matter how silly it is. It's for *you*. It's to help you to remember. Equally, the figure 26 may mean something to you: the number of your bus; the year you were born. And then it's easy to remember 26 36 46.

It's your imagination that provides the solution. But getting people to use their imagination (or remembering to use it!) is the problem.

Remembering telephone numbers

Again, by using association it becomes much easier to recall telephone numbers. There are certain numbers that are etched in our memories – those of relatives, friends, business contacts. But how often are you caught out because you can't remember a number? And so you don't make the call. Result: end of a relationship; lost business; friction. All because you didn't make a conscious effort to remember it.

So, again, firstly be interested in wanting to memorize the number. Then look for a way of remembering it by *relating* it to something *you already know*. Then, when you're trying to recall, your mind will twin the two things together.

For example, consider a number 021–3945. Your imagination provides you with a way of remembering 021 – perhaps how old you were when you graduated – and 3945 – the years in which the Second World War started and ended.

Would you have made these associations before reading this? So you've twinned a telephone number that you would like to recall at will, with facts you already know. You have programmed your mind. (Test: see if you can remember this number in 59 minutes time.)

Let's take another example: Beechwood 6549. For the exchange you could imagine a wooden table made of beechwood. Then think of retirement age being 65, and 49 was the year of your birth. Connect these together in your mind and see how easy it is. But remember. Be interested enough to *want* to remember it. (Test: see if you can remember this number in 60 minutes time.)

Note: when you've amazed yourself at how competent you've suddenly become at memorizing these example numbers, then jettison these from your psyche and substitute for them two telephone numbers that you want to remember (but as yet have never made the effort to do so).

Remembering names

The importance of remembering people's names has been discussed at length. The truth is, we're all capable of much more than we give ourselves credit for, when it comes to names.

If you were shown 150 photographs of celebrities from the entertainment world and public life, the chances are that you would be able to name upwards of 130 or more. And yet you probably have not met even one of these people. You recognized their faces *and* you remembered their names. The reason is that you're interested in retaining the name, and used (unconsciously) whatever associations you needed to remember the name. If you were shown a photograph of the actress Elizabeth Taylor in the role of Cleopatra, it's probably Cleopatra that makes you remember her name (or possibly the other way round).

The secret of remembering names again lies with each

individual. It's back to your own imagination. Certain names you will force yourself to remember simply because:

1 These people are important to your life. Of course you'll remember names of relatives, friends, work colleagues, important business clients, your doctor, possibly bank manager.
2 They were a great influence on your life: the name of the person who handed you the cheque for £200 000 for winning a lottery; your old headmaster or headmistress; the name of the driving examiner who enabled you to tear up your L plates after passing your driving test at the third attempt.

But what about the people we come across whose names we would like to remember, perhaps during a group business meeting or even at a social function? The problem's the same, although it may be more crucial in business.

Most names, at least surnames, can signify something to us. That is – we can equate them with something and paint word pictures. If you took the names Harper, Walker, Sheppard – they're easy. Others such as Longman, Royle, Bond, Silver – an association could easily be formed.

Now we must get one thing straight: your imagination belongs to you. What goes on in the top floor of your anatomy is your affair. If you devise daft methods of remembering names and it helps you, go ahead: make *your* day.

Let's take those names in turn:

Harper: you could picture this person playing a harp.
Walker: perhaps visualize this person with a rucksack.
Sheppard: sheep in his arms.
Longman: picture this person as a circus l-o-n-g man.
Royle: imagine this person with a crown on his head.
Silver: imagine this person with a patch over one eye.
Bond: picture this person as the famed 007.

Now if these examples don't prompt you to remember, then nothing will. Picture individuals in this way and make a point of registering the pictures in the mind. Then when you look at these people, it will be to the accompaniment of your finely tuned imagination. While they're frantically trying to remember your name, you are reeling off theirs; it trips off the tongue. And they just don't know how (it's just as well!).

But you know how. It's magic. The magic of memory.

7

Tricks with the telephone

As telecommunications become ever more sophisticated through increasingly advanced technology, that old-timer the telephone now tends to be taken for granted. But you must *never* underestimate – or overlook – its value in the first move of the selling game. It's the kick-off towards your goal. It conveys impressions. As such, your telephone self needs to be on top form.

Used wisely, the phone paves the way for successful meetings and can help you avoid long trips. If clients feel *comfortable* and reassured, in their dealings with you over the phone, then you're saving that most precious of commodities – time. Indeed, with the rising costs of key personnel, petrol costs and the general time constraints imposed on everybody, the telephone has now become the backbone of many operations. If you can use it to the greatest effect, the dividends are indisputable.

Problem: *some people just cannot communicate on the telephone.* There are some individuals, including so-called professionals, who seem to undergo a complete change of personality when confronted with a phone call. They can become stilted, nervous, incomprehensible, brusque, even rude, and will come across as plain 'hard going'. This is not very good when the aim is to sell (yourself).

Clients can also have bad telephone manners. This makes your job that much more difficult. Because you cannot see the person you're speaking to, you have no facial expressions or body language to *enforce* your message. That means you must make your voice work much harder than you would have to in a face-to-face situation.

How? By

1   *Choice of words*
2   *Tone of voice.*

People forget that a lot of the words they use when face to face are subconsciously chosen to go *with* a facial expression or gesticulation. This accompaniment gives added meaning to the words.

'How's the computer system we bought from you?'
'Terrible.'

   'Oh – I don't think I can possibly sign this.'

'You're a know-all, aren't you?'

All of these remarks could be *interpreted* quite differently over the phone without the normal wink or grin to signal humour. Facial expression can turn an 'insult' into a joke. Over the phone the astute listener would have to pick up voice inflections. He would be trying to establish whether a remark was a tease or was serious.

It feels unnatural to have to speak without using body language; that's why it's a lesson to watch experienced communicators conversing on the phone. They act naturally. You see them using facial expressions and gesticulating, just as if they were speaking face to face with the other person.

This puts feeling into the message, which is picked up at the other end of the line. Because acting out the conversation gives you the illusion of actually being there. It therefore makes your words more effective. You're not hampered by speaking into a plastic handset. And the changes of facial expressions automatically bring the right voice pattern. Try it.

Experiment: *try being angry over the phone with a big smile on your face*. Doesn't work, does it?

Exactly the same principles apply to training people to speak on radio. Professional trainers will invariably tell candidates to make their voices smile whenever appropriate in order to communicate enthusiasm or any other positive emotion. This gives colour and character to the unseen speaker's voice and makes its message more likely to be heard. Some companies give out stickers to employees with 'put a smile in your voice' to attach to the telephone. That's proof enough that people need to give more attention to their telephone techniques.

It's a misguided notion of feeling and looking silly that generally inhibits people smiling, scowling or whatever into a receiver. So they hide behind a monotone. They fail to understand that by using all the other means of expression you enhance your tone of voice and thus your delivery. And telephone is all about voice.

More often than not we are talking to 'strangers' on the telephone – people whom we've never met. And we're asking them to do things for us. We have to sell ourselves over the phone in order to get business with them under way.

What we say and *how* we deliver are the keys. You've only got to think of how *differently* you might respond to a request if delivered in contrasting ways. Consider how the following approaches would affect you:

1   Telephoning a doctor's receptionist for a home visit.

    'Hello. I want the doctor to come round this morning.' (More or less a demand)

'I know it's Monday morning and you're probably very busy, but I really do need the doctor to come round as soon as possible.' (A concerned manner, conveying that I'm looking at your point of view *too*)

2   Chasing up an insurance claim:

'I want my insurance claim settled immediately; it's two weeks since I sent it in.'

'It's two weeks since I sent my claim form in. I know there's been a Bank Holiday, but this is really causing me problems. Could you settle it quickly?' (Delivered with feeling)

It's obvious which approaches are going to get the best results over the telephone, isn't it?

Practically every day we find ourselves in the situation of having to ask something of somebody; so we have to sell them the idea of co-operating. In order to achieve the right response you have to sell yourself well.

In business, your first phone encounter will probably be with the secretary of the decision maker you want to reach. The secretary is subconsciously deciding how she feels about you. If the voice is pleasant and smiling (but not sycophantic!), that often gets you past the first hurdle. There's no pretence involved in smiling; if you went to the prospect's office and saw the secretary, you'd certainly be pleasant and smile. You happen to be present on the phone. What's the difference?

As a professional salesperson, you use the telephone to:

1   Find out information about the prospect's company.
2   Find out the name of the decision maker.
3   Talk to the decision maker.
4   Fix up a meeting (or, in many cases, effect a sale on the phone).

The process from start to finish has to be handled delicately. Firstly, you're asking someone (a stranger, by all accounts) to give you information. Then you're asking to speak to the person who would be concerned with your proposition.

The problem: there are too many people telephoning this busy individual to try to interest him in what they're selling. And a lot of these salespeople are bad news. They're just not professional in their approach. Result: buyers develop a cocoon around them. You can rarely get through to them directly. They're invariably '*in a meeting*', so say the protective secretaries, before asking you to 'write in'.

It's safe to say that the average businessman is constantly fighting against time. There aren't enough working hours in the day to deal with internal meetings and personnel problems, make out-of-town visits, read trade magazines and

meet salesmen. Time is at a premium. So if you manage to get connected to the decision maker – your story had better be good.

Take the stages of making a telephone approach to a company step by step. Your aim is to try to gauge whether they may be interested in your product, to find out whose 'domain' this falls into, and to get put through to the person if he is there. The stages are

1   Contact with switchboard operator.
2   Usually the decision maker's secretary (or someone else in the department).

If effective then:

3   Conversation with the decision maker.
4   Arranging a meeting with him (or sometimes a sale over the phone).

This scenario usually describes the origin of most eventual sales. So each process is crucial as a means to the end. If there is ineffective handling of the situation at any one stage, the whole thing collapses like a set of dominoes. The 'selling' doesn't start at stage 3; it starts right from stage 1!!

Look at the typical pattern.

Switchboard

This initial stage can sometimes be a real nightmare; it can really test your patience. As soon as you start you can find yourself getting nowhere fast:

Switchboard operator: 'Good morning – Oakley Securities – would you hold please.'

She may come back to you three minutes later with: 'Sorry to keep you. How can I . . . – just a moment, I have another call.'

Great, you think; what's wrong with *my* call! You didn't get a chance to say even one word.

Then there's the other type that allows you the privilege of a few words and cuts in once she's picked up a key word:

'Good morning – Tadwick Communications. How can I help you?'

'Morning. I'd like to know – for your salaries (click) . . . who would handle the computer software requirements?'

It's too late. The last bit died on your lips – you were transferred when you heard the click.

'Extension 228 – wages.'

'Oh – good morning. Computer systems for salaries – who handles this?'

'Nothing to do with us, mate. Who put you through?'

'Your switchboard.'

'I'll transfer you back.'

'Yes, but wait . . .' (click)

'Good morning – Tadwick Communications.'

'I spoke to you earlier. I wanted your computer systems people who handle . . .' (click)

'Morning – computer room, John speaking.'

'Oh, hello. I just wanted to speak to the person who handles the purchase of systems for payroll.'

'That wouldn't be us. Maybe you can try personnel, or I can transfer you to switchboard, they may be able to help.'

'No, no, please don't bother.' (click – *your* click)

Defeat. But it happens to us all. No wonder many salespeople hate and continually put off their telephone prospecting. It's not so much fear of rejection; it's fear of growing a *beard*!

Fortunately, not all operators are so hit-and-miss:

'Good afternoon – CBC International – how can I help you?'

'Good afternoon. *You could help me* by telling me who the travel manager is *these days*.'

Note:

1 It's difficult to refuse somebody assistance when you're offering help. Since she's offered it, you *subtly* remind her of this by starting with 'You could help me by . . .' (The 'How can I help you?' is a useful phrase that's crept over from the other side of the Atlantic, and is being used by many organizations now. But if *you* use it, be prepared to back it up.)

2 '. . . who the travel manager is *these days*.' This implies that you've dealt with the company before *and* that you knew the predecessor. This may or may not be. It doesn't matter. What matters is that the *split-second* evaluation in the operator's mind is that you've dealt with the company before (you may be a customer) and that accords you attention.

You needn't make it obvious to the initial contact that you're selling something. The harsh reality is that if you identify yourself as somebody after a sale, you risk being given the lowest priority – fobbed off. The goal is to get to the person who matters without being intercepted on the way. Blur the edges of your true intentions if it will get you through.

'The travel manager is Mr Jenkins.'

So you've found out who the travel manager is – but you still have to get past his secretary.

'Could I speak to him please?'
    'All calls go through to his secretary first.'
    'Oh. Could you tell me her name please?'
    'Yes, it's Sylvia.'

'Would you know her second name?'
'Yes. Wright – Sylvia Wright.'
Now you're through to the secretary.
'Mr Jenkins's office. Good afternoon.'
'Would that be Sylvia Wright?'
'Yes. Speaking.'

Secretary

It's back to the rewards of dealing in people's names, which was explored at length in Chapter 6.

You're massaging the ego. Most secretaries regard themselves as personal assistants to their bosses. Many have just such a title. Switchboard operators or receptionists may be unaware of this. Don't do what everybody else does and refer to her directly – as just a secretary. The connotations for a real PA with a key role will not endear you to her.

Address her as a person in her own right – with a name – and you will feel the immediate response. You've caught her attention. And psychologically she's predisposed towards you. You've confirmed her identity in the hierarchy – and people strive to do just that in the office jungle every day. (What's more, her boss may have given you her name, for all she knows.) The full name is more effective than using the formal Miss or Mr.

Now for the difficult part. You've confirmed *her* identity. Now try to establish *yours*. It's at this stage that many potential sales either fall by the wayside or take off. The trouble is that some individuals who screen calls for a busy boss take things too far. Their over-protectiveness can mean that their bosses don't get to hear about something that could be of interest. You have to increase your efforts to ensure that you get a hearing with the actual decision maker.

There are certain prerequisites:

Courtesy   There's no substitute. We like talking to personable, well-mannered people. There's a shortage. So if you show it, you're half-way there. What about the other half? *Do you sound important?* Unfortunately it's a fact that you're far more likely to get through if you're a VIP than Charlie Brown, the sales executive; but you'll also have more chance of being put through if you sound as though you know what you're talking about. Be confident, but not overly so. All right, you *are* important; that's not the point at issue. Do you *sound* important? That's all the screener has got to go by. She can't assess your outward appearance on the telephone, it's the sound of you that you're judged on. What you say and how you say it.

Let's continue. You've just asked if Mr Jenkins is free.

'Could you tell me what it's in connection with?'
   'Yes, of course. It's MBI Programmes. My name's Harrison, I have to discuss a conference package with him.'
   'Has he spoken to you before, Mr Harrison?'
   'No – we haven't spoken yet.'
   'I'll see if he's free.'
   After two minutes: 'He's rather tied up at the moment – could you write in, perhaps?'
   'It's not that simple. I need to actually discuss the starting point with him. Miss Wright, I don't mind holding on. I only need four or five minutes of his time.'
   'Just a moment, Mr Harrison.'
   'Jenkins speaking.'

She's let you through the filter. Well done. But don't forget that the bosses themselves can also relish playing hard to get!! They feel *powerful* when they refuse to take calls. It gives them a sense of satisfaction. (People want to talk to me, but I just haven't got the time.) They also think it necessary to keep impressing upon their secretaries that they're not prepared to talk to all and sundry.
   But there's no denying the fact that assistants wield great

influence. You have to sell yourself to them *first* by being courteous and sounding important. Look at it from their point of view. They don't want to look inefficient to their boss. They have to be *selective* about who is allowed access. In reality, some carry this too far. So it's up to the salesperson to create the right impression and then to persist – pleasantly.

The boss usually asks his secretary for a thumbnail evaluation (30 seconds) of the intruder on the phone and what the call is about. Then it's up to her to sell him the idea of talking to you (*it's strange how everybody seems to be selling!*).

Chatting up the decision maker

When you eventually get through to the person you're aiming for, you are effectively a guest on his telephone line; you should conduct your conversation with that in mind.

You've certainly interrupted this individual in the middle of something. You don't know what kind of mood he's in. He could be at the height of a crisis. He may have just come back from an overseas trip that morning. He could be recovering from an illness. He might be in the middle of a meeting. His house might have burnt down the previous night. But whatever it is, you can be sure he won't tell you. It's up to you now. Use some empathy – the thing that most people are short of. Get inside the mind.

'Mr Jenkins – thank you for your time. I'll be brief.'

Two brownie points out of two. Well, you've acknowledged he's busy. That's courteous. Secondly, you've made a positive move towards ensuring that you get his attention while you're talking. You've promised to be *brief*. What music to his ears!

You know how it is. Somebody comes on the line. You've got a million things to do. If you know that person prattles on, your mind says: 'Oh no, not him again.' Consequently you switch off, and all the time the caller is speaking you're distracted because you're trying to work out which sentence will be the last. So you miss most of what's being said.

So often, people take a phone call from a salesman under sufferance. Either because they find it difficult to say no, or because they've refused many times before and feel they ought to kill it dead. It's a negative situation from the start. It becomes more of a fencing match.

But when the salesperson says 'I'll be brief', the prospect is more likely to drop his guard. He can actually afford to pay attention and listen; he can relax a little and actually hear what's being said. Who knows – he might even buy!

Certain types of people prefer you to get to the point quickly. Their own minds race away with what's being discussed, and it's no good you being left on the starting block. (This particular type will feature in a later chapter.)

Many salespeople prolong a telephone call by speaking in a slow monotone, throwing out sentences and failing to finish them because they've thought of something else. Their conversations go something like this: 'Maybe we can try and . . . I mean if you want to change your fleet over the next – um . . . perhaps we should really be . . .' And it goes on and on. There are people like this around. And they actually have the nerve to talk to prospects over the phone. They utter a monologue of several unfinished sentences: no beginning, no end, *no sale*.

You might get away with this in a face-to-face situation where you may be seen to have compensatory qualities. But, of course, on the phone you rely solely on the projection of your message.

Come on. Get inside the mind. What's happening on the other end of the line?

At the other end of the line

It happens to everybody, all the time. You may be at home, in absolute agony: *will Sue Ellen get back with JR* – no, don't do it, don't believe him, he wants you back in the sanatorium . . .

The telephone rings. You turn down the volume control on the TV. Cursing the interruption, you force yourself to the phone. A brusque 'hello'.

'Oh – is that you John? It's Tom here.'

'Tom – hi.'

'You sounded different. Anyway, listen. I had to ring you. Remember we were talking about that hotel in Portugal the other night . . . oh, just a minute John – get away, Samantha, daddy's on the phone. No, you can't . . . look, go and find mummy, she's got something for you. Sorry John – interruptions *all* the time. Now where was I – how's things anyway? OK?'

'Yeah – yeah. Not bad.' (mega brusque)

'Can you remember the name of that hotel then John?'

'What hotel?'

The conversation continues in the same vein.

This kind of situation occurs every day in business and social life.

Can you imagine Tom, after the call, when his wife says: 'Well – how's John then?'

'Mmm – he was a bit strange.'

'Oh. What d'you mean by strange?'

'Well. He was a bit brusque – not his usual pleasant self.'

'You don't think Joanna's left him?'

'No, no.'

'Maybe we've upset him. You don't owe him any money, do you? Or have we borrowed something that we haven't returned?'

'No. Anyway, he definitely was a bit odd. Unusual for him though. He didn't seem to be paying attention to what I was saying – just wasn't interested.'

'Well – maybe they had company. Did you ask him?'

'No. Hey – you could be right – when he hung up hurriedly towards the end, he did mention something about a *Sue Ellen*.'

What a situation. Both parties are left feeling disturbed by the call. John is cursing Tom, and Tom is inwardly annoyed with John ('Well – if he wants to be like that, forget it'). Later on, after the programme, John may analyse his telephone conversation (what conversation?) and think to himself: 'Mmmm, maybe I was a bit short with Tom. No – he wouldn't have taken offence.'

The problem is very simple. When you telephone somebody, at work or at home, you are *bound to be interrupting them in something*: writing a report, gardening, eating, watching television, having a row. But some interruptions are much worse than others.

Just imagine if Tom had used his head to get inside John's mind:

'Hello.' (brusque)

Tom picks up the rather curt greeting. He can't be offended; it's not directed at him. John doesn't yet know who

is calling; so it's a general signal that suggests impatience.

'John – it's Tom here. Am I interrupting something? Can you talk?'

'Well, it's OK. I'm just watching Dallas; it's the last episode of this series.'

'Hey, listen – I'll call you back at nine. It's not life or death. Talk to you later.'

'But . . .'

'No, listen. Don't worry. Talk to you at nine. Bye for now.'

What a different scenario to the previous one. John is impressed by Tom showing such empathy. You can bet he'll be the one to make the call at 9 p.m. before Tom does. And he'll be all ears too.

People don't concentrate on what you're saying if their minds are elsewhere. You're being two-timed again. It can't be repeated often enough. The effectiveness of your message over the phone will be at its optimum only if the other party is paying full attention.

Most people don't let on that you're interrupting them or that you've caught them at a bad time. It's up to *you* to detect it from the tone of voice; remember, telephone is all about voice. Then you decide what to do. But you take the lead; it's in your interest.

The volume of business conducted by telephone every day demands expertise in the art of faceless contact. The convenience of long-distance telephone lines has encouraged less travel and fewer face-to-face encounters. Your success in winning business thus depends more and more on your performance on the telephone. And knowing *when* and *when not* to speak can decide the outcome of your proposition.

If you catch a person at the wrong time, it could be the end of your sale, pay rise, trip to the Hanover fair, new desk, day's holiday or whatever. And you don't usually get a second chance. Remember the point made earlier: people don't generally like to change their minds after a refusal. It makes them look indecisive and appear wrong in the first instance. Even if they know that is so, they stick rigidly to their original decision, which may have been made hastily. Why was it made in haste? Because they were busy and wanted to get rid of the person. Now if that person had picked up these vibes and offered to call back – well, that could be a different story.

So. *Timing* is all-important. If you pick up from a strained voice that it's not convenient and therefore unconducive, then nip the conversation in the bud. Sometimes the other party does it, but it will usually have to be you. You have more to lose.

Using the telephone effectively is an art. You've got to make sure you make a firm connection – that you find the right wavelength.

Ringing when the client has company

Quite often when you call your client or prospect, he is with somebody. He may tell you so, and suggest that either one of you rings back later:

'I'm in the middle of a meeting at the moment. Can I call you back?'

'I have someone with me. Can you call back later?'

If, as in the first example, he offers to call you back, say that *you* will call. It's better that way. He is quite likely to forget. You will save yourself waiting and wondering. Even if he hasn't forgotten, phoning you will be low priority (with all the problems that have emerged from his meeting). It's at basement level in his action tray.

You're lucky if the prospect does tell you that he's with someone and that he'd like to talk later. More often than not you won't be told. That's where the trouble starts.

Problem: *people talk differently on the phone when some-one is with them.* The reasons include:

1 *They are nervous.*
2 *They want to impress.*
3 *They're conscious that they're keeping the person(s) with them waiting.*
4 *They don't want the person present to know about the topic being discussed.*
5 *They're speaking through an intercom phone (and their 'audience' can hear your every word).*

Catch yourself when you are alone, talking in the privacy of your own office. Your telephone conversation is probably quite fluent, as you gaze at your familiar surroundings. You don't have to watch what you say at your end. Nobody can hear you. It's a private conversation between two people.

Now compare this situation to one in which a person or a group of people is sitting with you. You probably adopt a more officious tone; you are less friendly. Your words are chosen more carefully, so you are less natural and less fluent. You're conscious that your dialogue is being vetted by the other person(s).

If you are telephoning somebody for the first time, to try to gain his interest, and he happens to have somebody with him, you could have problems. He may be the type that's always ready to impress the person present. So he may try to 'kick you around'. It's done for show. His audience sees a flexing of corporate clout that says: 'I know how to handle time wasters – people trying to sell me things.'

You may be a nice guy. Your telephone manner may be excellent, your proposition good. But there'll be an artificial rejection of your call because your contact wants to look clever and powerful in front of his onlookers.

If your prospect is having a meeting of some sort in his office, then a phone call forces a break in the proceedings.

Meetings have various levels of importance. He could be in with his secretary, partners, chairman, advertising agency, liquidator. Now it would be fine if he told you to call back. But many people don't, often because they think it will be an inconvenience (to you or to him).

If he does take your call, his concentration is *wavering* because he's aware of keeping the people in his office waiting. Their time is valuable too. The easiest way to get you off the line is to say no to whatever you're proposing. *Regardless.*

Sometimes your call concerns something which has already been discussed and is confidential. He doesn't want the person present to know that he's thinking of buying an office jacuzzi, or an apartment in Marbella. His conversation with you thus becomes stilted and monosyllabic. You think he's not interested anymore.

It's important to learn that, when a prospect has company, you have to read from the tone of voice whether you should *risk* a quick shot at your proposition or wait for a more favourable opportunity.

If you're speaking to somebody for the first time, it's as well to ask if it's convenient to talk. Even if you've passed through the filter and he's agreed to speak, this gesture can make the prospect more responsive. *When making telephone contact, it's so important to assess whether the time is right to put forward your proposition, or whether you would get a better hearing at some other time.*

How many times have you come off the phone and thought to yourself: 'That's strange. He was interested when we met last week; what could have happened? He sounded completely different . . . tense almost . . .' He probably sounded different and less receptive because he had people present. You should have picked up the vibes and cut it short. If you risk having your say regardless when telephoning a new prospect for the first time, and it's the wrong moment, you are likely to lose out on this occasion and not be given another opportunity.

The moral: if you're in any doubt, ask whether it's *convenient to talk*. You're getting inside the mind. You're showing off your ESP (empathy, sincerity, perspicacity): here we go again!

Timing is so important in the persuasion game. We will often respond to the *same* offer completely differently at different *times*; it's human nature. It should be stressed again and again: bringing something up at the wrong time can lay it to rest forever. Whereas waiting until the right opportunity can lead you straight to your goal.

Many sales are lost because the salesman cannot understand the need to be *intuitive* before pitching on the phone. Would you ring up your prospect at 9.15 a.m. on his first morning back from his two-week summer holiday (about the proposition that you discussed on the eve of his departure)? Would you call your boss, the managing director, about your adventurous choice of new car, on the morning that he discovers that the company is the subject of an unwelcome takeover bid?

All other things being equal, people respond better if they're in a good mood and not under pressure, and when things are generally going well. They'll be more inclined to give their best attention. As salespeople we should constantly be aware of this and use it to our advantage. We know it's true. We're exactly the same.

Talking your way into an appointment

You've got through to Mr Jenkins now. So take things one step at a time. You know that when you use somebody's name, your whole approach becomes that much more personal.

Now you want the other person to remember *your* name and your company's name – or at worst, one out of the two. Research has shown that people contacted by a salesperson by phone are more embarrassed about missing the company name than that of the caller. They don't mind asking for your name at the end of the call.

The problem is that most salespeople, on getting through to Mr Right, blurt out as one elongated phrase (often mumbled): 'Hello, it's James Harrison of MBI International here. I'd like to discuss ways and means of improving ... '(no pause for breath). Almost as if ashamed sometimes, salespeople feel obliged to speak as fast as possible – to get the petty details out of the way. Petty? Your name, the company's name? Hardly.

Get this straight. You have got something that could potentially help the prospect – and his organization (in *that* order). What are you embarrassed about? You're in business. He's in business. Snap: you're both businessmen. *You're equal*.

The attitude of apologizing for the names is of no use to you as a salesperson. You then become fodder for the prospect on the other end of the line. He may well take advantage of your lack of self-esteem. You will certainly lack respect in his eyes. There's every reason not to be apologetic. A potential client would often rather that you justified his time (and your own) spent in speaking to you on the phone, and that you persuaded him to see you. After all – nobody likes to miss out. You might have some interesting ideas.

So when you introduce yourself by phone to a stranger, be aware of how much his mind can take in all at once. You want your identity firmly established. So say it s-l-o-w-l-y: 'Mr Jenkins. Good morning.' Pause. 'It's MBI here.' Pause again. Let him assimilate and remember. Let his mental computer do a rapid search for recognition. Now the first bit has sunk in, you can state your name: My name's James Harrison.'

Think about it. You give the person a chance to either recall or register the name of your company. Then you give him the opportunity to hear your name and therefore remember it. Result: he doesn't feel as if he's just talking to a *voice*. That's better for you. *It's easy to reject a voice*, harder to reject a *person*.

Just think of a call you've had from somebody who rattles off his name and organization. If you're preoccupied you may have missed both pieces of information. You don't feel any rapport with the person speaking and, as you're busy anyway, the inclination is: *how do I get this voice off my line*?

To recap. You've said you'll be brief; the prospect has computed that. You've given the name of your organization; he's computed that. And then your name; hopefully he'll remember it, but, if not, it's easy for him to say later on in the conversation: 'I'm sorry, I didn't catch your name.' It's slightly more subtle than asking: 'What's the name of your company again?' Prospects don't like to appear lax. It puts them off forming a business relationship with you, if they don't feel on top. So it's up to you to make it easy on them.

There's every chance too that if you enunciate clearly and

pace your words the listener will feel like writing down these details while you're passing them on.

Right. You've sorted out the identity problem. Now see if you can arouse interest in your services and perhaps arrange a meeting. But remember that before people will agree to see you, they want to be reasonably sure about some key points:

1 They like the sound of *you* (and therefore of what you stand for).

2 The product shows promise. Therefore they're not wasting time that could be better spent on a pressing report, important meeting, playing golf, or whatever. There is sacrifice involved, after all.

3 *You would be easy to get rid of, if they didn't want to buy.* This is a very important consideration, and cannot be stressed too much. Many salespeople never get that elusive meeting because of their pushy attitude over the phone. The prospect thinks: if I can't get this person off the phone, what would he be like once he'd infiltrated my office? So although he may well be interested, he is dubious about granting an entrée to the salesperson.

Nobody really likes saying no – especially in person. It's easier on the telephone; one can fence, say 'Send me some literature' and end the matter there. When the salesperson telephones to follow up, he is told by the secretary that her boss has looked at it and isn't interested at the moment, 'but we'll put it on file and . . .'. The Hollywood equivalent is: 'Don't call us, we'll call you!'

So it's important to remember that the prospect wants to feel comfortable about *being able to say no* after a face-to-face meeting. If he senses he'd be dealing with an aggressive, pushy type, he'd rather go for the 'write to me' option.

You can see then that it's how you come across on the phone that determines whether or not you get an audience with the person you are after. If you show that you're willing to invest time and you're not going to push him into a corner, you've got a good chance. Not only of seeing him – but also of selling to him.

Yet so many people fail to get appointments because they cannot see the reasoning of this psychology. They mistake *aggression* for confidence. There's nothing wrong with being confident about what you're selling; in fact it's a prerequisite. But there's a thin line between just enough confidence and too much.

They also mistake *enthusiasm* for confidence. Again, there's nothing wrong with being enthusiastic. But some people go over the top. It gives the whole conversation an air of falsity. It puts the buyer off. He ends up refusing to see the salesperson. He's thinking: 'I wouldn't mind knowing about this service – could be useful. But this guy's irritating. I'm sure the product's good – but it's not *that* good! I'll never get rid of him if I see him; he'll hound me.' It's the salesman's attitude that's done this. He hasn't sold himself well. Did he get inside the mind? No. The buyer's turned off. For the wrong reasons. And that's tragic.

When the salesman in our example said at the beginning of the telephone call that the conversation would be short, that made the prospect relax. Now how about the same tactic when trying to arrange a first meeting? Consider:

'I understand, Mr Jenkins, that you're in charge of paging systems and cellular technology, for your company.'

'Yes I am.'

'We're a telecommunications company. I've a feeling we met at a seminar about a couple of years ago.'

'MBI did you say? Yes, I remember. Somewhere in the Cotswolds.'

'Of course – that super country house hotel just outside Gloucester. Hatton Court.'

'That's it. I remember the bar well – they serve beer from twenty-seven different countries!'

'Quite. I'm calling because I'd like to fix up a short meeting – half an hour or so. Ideally, within the next two weeks.'

'Well – this week's bad. Next week . . . let me see: any day except Tuesday and Thursday morning.'

'OK. How about Monday, three o'clock?'

'That's fine. I'm writing it in my diary now – MBI Ltd – Mister . . .?'

'Harrison – James Harrison.'

'Right, Mr Harrison – see you then. Nice to have spoken to you. Thank you for calling.'

'Thank you. Look forward to the ninth at three o'clock.'

Very conciliatory. If only more calls were like that. But the point is this: we can *steer* them in that direction by understanding how people's minds work.

Analyse: '*a short meeting – half an hour or so*' As well as being music to Jenkins's ears, it delivers a double message to the mind:

1   The salesman is implying about himself: *my* time is *valuable* too, because I'm successful. And I'm successful because I'm good.
2   My exit will be painless. You won't have to get rid of me; I don't have that much time anyway. So *relax* when we meet.

If those two factors don't encourage the prospect to be interested – and perhaps buy – nothing will.

Analyse: '*Ideally, within the next two weeks.*' Notice the flexibility of the meeting date. The word 'ideally' on its own suggests – no pressure. But it's a subtle indication of your preference.

If you follow a similar procedure to the one outlined, you've certainly done everything you can to help him *buy* the appointment.

What often happens at the eventual meeting? The meeting

goes on for longer than half an hour – but not at *your* instigation, at the other person's. The relaxed prospect ends up asking all sorts of questions. And after he's agreed to buy from you, he apologizes to you on the way out – for taking up too much of *your* time!

8

Client types

It may be unfair to typecast, but there are certain types of individuals whom you find yourself coming up against time and again in your search for new business.

We're all a blend of different types, but in a business context there are some real stereotypes who can be readily categorized. Identifying the type allows you to adopt the appropriate techniques for handling that person. You've almost certainly met some or all of these following five types.

Get on with it: give me the bottom line

Relatively easy to make an appointment

This type is willing to give most people a chance if he approves of their initial approach. Somebody who didn't waste too much of his time on the telephone, for instance, would probably be granted a meeting.

This type likes to keep up with what's going on. He's concerned that the competition might be using you, and so he might be missing out. This makes him want to know more.

Coffee comes within three minutes

It's been ordered well in advance and is brought in by a secretary with an endless smile. He probably has his own mug, with some sort of inscription on it (ego boosting), bought for him by someone in the office.

If you finish your coffee in the first ten minutes, it's easier to get thrown out; so take your time. The prospect who turns out to be only half-interested may well only grant you as much time as it takes to drink your coffee. It gives him an indication of the earliest point at which he can terminate the meeting.

You can unnerve this type if he thinks that you have temporary control over the proceedings. If you want to stay, then sip imaginary mouthfuls from your cup (like they do in 'Dynasty'!)

Talks quickly

This is symptomatic of the rest of his character. Time is constantly on his mind. In fact he probably looks at his watch at regular intervals while he talks to you. He doesn't make any attempt to do it surreptitiously; he's blatant about it. *His* time is being spent; *your's* doesn't enter into the equation.

For this type of person, *time is the new currency*. 'I can't spend too much time . . .' is one of his frequent sayings. His secretary judges the status of his visitors by how much time he has *spent* with them. Time has become a fashionable measure of success.

Studies you intently

He maintains a steely eye contact with you (when not looking at his Rolex) while you're speaking. He's listening only for key words. The rest of the time he's checking you out: your speech, mannerisms, clothes, signs of nervousness.

Desk shows a lot of activity

Because he likes to be in on the action, his desk is covered with a lot of visual noise (that's why he'll sometimes meet you in the boardroom). Small wonder he doesn't like wasting time. If he sat around seeing people like you all the time, he wouldn't be visible from your side of the desk.

Wants you to get to the point quickly

This is the essential hallmark of this type. He likes people who cut through the flannel and are succinct and sincere. He's worldy-wise enough to know what is what; so he wants the sell to be straight. If he senses sales patter he starts to show signs of impatience.

   If that's allowed to happen, then you're sunk. This type of person is thinking of a thousand things at once anyway; so if you ramble on, he'll just switch to the other 999 things on his mind!

Essentially, this type can be a blessing to deal with if your pitch is right and he has an interest in your product. He will always want to buy 'you' first; and if that hurdle is overcome, he will deal with you on his terms. The fact that you got to the bottom line quickly indicates that you value your time too. He definitely appreciates this quality in others. You know where you stand with a person like this.

This type of person achieved his present position by sorting out the wheat from the chaff – and that includes the likes of you.

Aggressive: what's in it for me?

Heavy security

You were probably subjected to the third degree before getting the appointment. You may have had the initial 'Can you write in?' from his secretary or assistant. But your persistence got you through to him, and he agreed to see you (under sufferance). He emphasized the fact that he couldn't promise anything.

You're guilty until proven innocent

With this type, you're observed suspiciously from the start. You're made to feel very much like an intruder when you enter his domain. This is designed to make you feel uncomfortable. He wants the upper hand. He'd like to see you crack. If you did, you'd probably offer him a better deal.

Knows all about your company (or so he thinks)

He claims to know a great deal about you from his colleagues, previous dealings and other vague sources. He actually knows very little – but he has these set preconceived ideas. He is therefore reluctant to listen attentively, and nods continuously to indicate 'Yes, I know; yes, I know.'

It turns out that he has often confused your company with another. So all his criticisms and views are wrongly directed at you. If you discover this during the meeting and point out the case of mistaken identity, you risk making him lose face. So you suffer because he couldn't be bothered to check his facts beforehand.

Suffers from desk aggression

Psychologists have long recognized the change that comes over certain people when they get behind the steering wheel of a car. Thoughtful, kind human beings often become menacing and aggressive. 'Driver aggression' is a term that's been coined.

Put some people behind a desk and you get an almost parallel situation: let's call it '*desk aggression*'. It gives this type a feeling of power and causes a personality change. The

bigger the desk, the bigger the transformation that takes place.

Try and get this type *away* from his power base if there's alternative seating. It will alter the outcome of your meeting.

Looks for ways of tripping you up

Basically, he didn't really want to see you. But you persisted. So it's a case of – come into my parlour for some Chinese torture.

He'll try to catch you out during your discourse. His ego tells him that whatever he is doing at the moment, he's doing it right. He doesn't need what you're offering. Why introduce another variable into the equation and upset the balance? He's thinking: 'What's in it for me? No thanks. I'll stick with the current suppliers; they're not brilliant, but who needs a change? Besides – that was a wonderful case of Scotch they sent me last Christmas.'

Criticizes prices and other features

This type invariably finds fault with your pricing policy and product specifications. All the time there is an ego-based justification for sticking with the status quo. He will refuse to accept that the way he has been operating could be improved upon. So he goes through all the features of your product and demolishes them. Any valid resistance by you to his claims is bulldozed.

Wants trial products for virtually nothing

He buys a small amount from you at low cost (if you let him) with the promise of big business if it's favourably received. You could end up waiting forever.

He's now had the opportunity of trying you out practically for free. He can brag to his boss about it. If it works, fine. If it doesn't, well, there's not much of a financial loss – and it's proved his point. Besides, he can use this situation to keep his present suppliers on their toes and get better service from them. The threat of changing supplier works wonders. You end up doing him a big favour. And this type deserves it the least.

This sort will try to manipulate you from the word 'go'. Keep your cool. He may end up conceding if you can maintain your position. The fact that you've refused to budge too much, indicates in his eyes that you've got something to offer. Now he's more interested.

General advice for tackling this type of buyer: use your head (and wear a crash helmet!). Be prepared for a few knocks.

Meticulous and methodical

Don't be a minute late

You're dealing with somebody whose life is highly organized. He is usually an older person, and has probably been with the organization for many years. He's very much dyed in the wool.

When you fixed the meeting he was very specific about time (11.40 a.m.) and probably insisted on giving you directions (even though you told him not to bother as you once worked opposite his offices). Just hear him out. If you don't you'll offend. His working life revolves around detail; don't try and change it.

You're due at 11.40, and the meeting will certainly not last longer than 12.20. At that time his secretary will come in with a finger bowl just as he's taken his cheese sandwich and orange from his briefcase. Don't even think of interrupting this ritual.

Doesn't like people who talk fast.

Slow down your speech with this type. Things have to be conducted at a certain pace – *his* pace. If you talk fast he thinks you're trying to gloss over certain points, and the tag of 'fast-talker' takes on its worst connotations.

Long pauses when he talks to you

He's a cautious person generally – and this applies to his choice of words. Consequently he s-t-r-e-t-c-h-e-s everything out, and there are long pauses in mid sentence. It's difficult to know when to start talking, because you don't know when he's finished discussing a particular point.

If you interrupt him inadvertently, he'll never forgive you. You think he's finished his sentence; then, *just when you thought it was safe to go back into the conversation,* . . .!!

Checked out all your competitors

It's a by-product of his nature that he has to have all relevant facts and assess all possible alternatives before making up his mind.

In your case that means evaluating all of your rivals; so you had better be clued up on what they offer. He won't tell you what he can get from the others; on the contrary. That's one of the reasons why he s-t-r-e-t-c-h-e-s everything out; there's less chance of him accidentally giving anything away. He knows what else is available, and his filing cabinet will testify to that. He doesn't so much have files on potential suppliers – more like huge dossiers.

He mentally conducts a 'for and against' for all the benefits you put forward, compared with the competition. If you're the first person he's seen in your field, then he'll start calling in the competition one by one. So you can't win by being first with this type of person.

Wants straight answers

When he asks you a question, make sure you answer it (this is not the time or place to practise for a future in politics). His mind is programmed to receive a reply. Without one, the computer cannot go on to the next instruction.

Wants everything in writing

After the meeting he will insist that everything you've discussed be put in writing (I hope you made lots of notes!). This is not necessarily a buying signal, as with other types of buyer. It is more of a safety valve (for him) should he actually decide to talk to you again – or even buy from you. He needs a résumé of what you actually said.

Unfortunately, the lack of spontaneity from this type means that you very rarely get an agreement or order at the initial meeting. Much of your face-to-face impact is *lost*

.... just when you thought it was safe....

because of having to go away and put everything discussed in writing. The sad thing is that this sort of person *forgets* most of the original discussion and now remembers only what the letter points out. Also, his seeing so many other suppliers means that he confuses one individual with another; that is hopeless for you.

It's very much in his hands now. You can't force another meeting, and at best you can hope that he contacts you again. So your letter must be effective. Reiterate the good points you made; don't dwell on his objections. It's up to *him* to remember those. Cover most of the important points. Always remember that he's probably going to discuss this with somebody else in the organization – and that person hasn't even seen you. So your letter has to sell.

If possible, it can help to leave out a fairly important piece of information and suggest in the letter that he contact you if he needs clarification. The secret is not to give everything. You need a reason for the prospect to get back to you. And when he does, you can ask if the contents of the letter were clear. At least you then get an opportunity to put him right on some things he may have misinterpreted. That can make all the difference between a rejection and a sale.

Calls you back to meet a third party

If he asks you back for another meeting, he will probably bring in somebody else. It may be the person who will ultimately be using the product. His instinct for playing safe means that he wants approval from the third party. Or, as is probably more often the case in business and job interviews, he wants to be able to dilute the *blame* if things don't turn out quite right.

Try to work out what type this other person is and handle him accordingly. But remember that the ultimate decision maker is your original contact Mr Methodical. Aim to get the third party to sell to him. Let him take the reins.

Wants references of satisfied customers

If Mr Methodical decides to buy, he will first want you to supply the names of some customers that he could talk to. In reality, such referees are rarely contacted. The request is a reassurance that you can confidently proffer some names. That's usually enough.

Remember that essentially you're dealing here with a *pedant*. If you can recognize this difficult type and have the patience and understanding to cope with him, you can get results. But make sure your product is good. This type can be a pain if he buys from you and then has cause for complaint. Have your air ticket ready!

Friendly: I'll talk to anybody

Very receptive to your phone call

When you first telephone, he's quite easygoing and very attentive. If he's interested he sells *you* the idea of a meeting between the two of you (makes a nice change).

Calls you by your first name on arrival

He disposes of formalities and, being the friendly sort, immediately calls you by your given name. He perhaps asks you to call him Tom, Dick or whatever.

Has unconventional seating arrangement in his offfice

His office is very homely; it's an extension of him. His desk is intended for *his* use only; it is tucked away at the far corner of the room facing the wall. He doesn't like discussions from his desk; it's too territorial, and not fair on the other person. Besides, the papers and clutter there would prevent him from giving undivided attention to his visitors. (This is a godsend to you; remember Chapter 5?)

You sit on a couch – very relaxed. 'Take your jacket off, if you like' he offers.

Talks a lot initially

When you first meet, he talks a lot to put you at ease. He speaks with animated gestures and facial expressions that say 'I'm enjoying life' and also 'I'm enjoying our conversation' (but you haven't said anything yet!).

Asks you about your personal life

This guy just shows a keen friendly interest in you. He's a people person; he makes no bones about it. His initial vibes tell him that you're a nice person to deal with; so he's finding out more about you. He asks about your hobbies and interests, and looks for common ground. He leaves discussion about business until much later; he's still buying *you*.

Likes to hear about your other customers

Name dropping of some of your existing customers goes down well. He likes dealing with companies that have customers known to him. He feels no need to check out your company.

Don't mention any company that you're currently having trouble with for whatever reason. It doesn't matter how impressive a name it is. He may be acquainted with them and may receive negative feedback. It would be unfair on you to be judged in this way.

Gives you his agreement to buy quickly

He likes to tell you almost *immediately* whether he's interested or not. He doesn't believe in playing games once he's bought you. You've passed the test. Here's your certificate (order form), signed at the bottom. He actually values *your* time *as well as* his own.

Of course, it has to be a pleasure dealing with this sort of person. This type invites empathy – and if you've got it, you can hardly fail. It is undoubtedly the ideal type to deal with. There are a few of them around, but they're not that easy to find.

Amicable: let's get you off your guard

Finally, there is a variation of the friendly type that is worth mentioning. His friendliness is motivated by self-interest – to lull you into revealing information.

Pleasant welcome when you arrive

You are greeted by your first name and made to feel like a long-lost friend.

Seating is on a comfortable sofa

Again this is similar to the previous type.

Keen to know your status in the company

He studies your business card closely; he wants to gauge your seniority. He asks how long you've been with the organization. He wants to know whether you have the clout to make a decision on a deal (that he's carefully thought out *before* you arrived) or whether you'd have to get the approval of a superior back at the office. If he works out that you do have ultimate authority, you will probably be offered biscuits with your coffee.

By establishing your length of service with the company, he may just be ensuring that he's dealing with someone experienced. That's quite in order. So he's checking out your credentials. And if he's not happy, you may have a very short meeting. ('What, he's only been in the business for three months? I've been in it twenty-eight years. He can't tell me anything. I'll cancel the coffee.')

If you feel that it would turn the buyer off to know that you've been in your present employment for only a short time, make sure you allude to your previous experience. But if you are confident and it shows, it usually dispels any doubt.

Tries to make you feel relaxed and off guard

This type knows that most selling situations are in formal surroundings, with buyer and seller going through the set motions. Such a situation tends to make the salesman cautious about how much he gives away – not just in terms of price, *but also of product limitations*.

So the buyer knows that by departing from the norm and making you feel relaxed and open in conversation, he's likely to get a little bit more out of you – and more. And maybe even more. Who knows, you may even tell him some secrets about *his* competitors. But he could just be testing you. If you rat on his rivals then you would probably let them in on *his* business secrets. ('So. Thanks for the information about my competitors; it'll come in very handy. And by the way – no sale.')

This friendly type also knows that if you are relaxed, you're likely to bend that bit more in a negotiating situation. After all, if the salesman is made to feel well received, he's likely to make an extra effort to offer a good deal.

This type of buyer is calculating. So make sure that even in such relaxed surroundings, you remain totally in control. The buyer is hoping to put you in an *expansive mood*. If you falter at all, he'll seize on this as a chance to take advantage. So remain alert. If you give him a good deal, let him see it's a *deliberate* decision and not the result of weakening under pressure. He'd rather deal with somebody strong minded.

Of course, most people are a cocktail of the various types. However, understanding different behavioural features and mentally classifying those so afflicted (or blessed!) will be an enormous aid in using your ESP techniques.

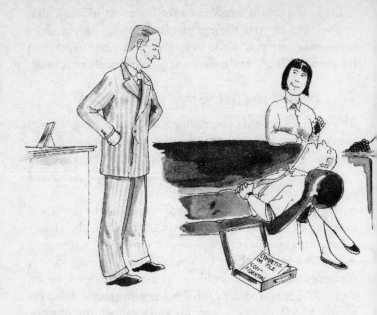

With most types there is a little bit of *another* type trying to get out. You can encourage that with your line of questioning. But what techniques you use will also depend on *your* type.

9

Stereotype salespeople

In Chapter 8 we discussed various types of client. Here we identify four stereotypical salespeople.

Rambles on regardless

On arrival, discusses journey/parking ad nauseam

This type can't help himself. He feels compelled to comment on road or weather conditions as an easy opener, either because he is nervous or because he can't think of anything else to say.

Of course, it's all right to remark on the ups and downs of your journey; in fact, the prospect may even ask. But keep it brief. That's not the point of the meeting. We presume he's busy; so get on with it.

Carries a large synthetic executive case

His bulging case smacks of that dying species, the commercial traveller. It contains masses of literature, handbooks, biros, a shoe horn and so on. The sight of such a case can be a turn-off to the prospect. He doesn't want a hard time. What's going to come out of this Pandora's box?

Floods the prospect's desk with literature

He assumes the prospect is a graduate of the rapid reading school, and starts by overloading him with company literature, testimonials and statistics. He's latched on to what he heard said during his sales induction that 'A picture paints a thousand words'; timing was never mentioned. So he does the same thing on every visit like an automaton.

Talks to prospect while he is trying to read

Ugh! It's bad enough with the prospect trying to wade through all that bumf. Worse, as he tries to read the salesman is wittering away. The prospect doesn't know what to concentrate on. Should he be listening *or* looking at literature? Who knows? Nobody knows.

Pays no regard to time

This type of salesman doesn't attempt to find out how much time the prospect has before his next engagement. He rambles on regardless. He is intent only on how much time he has to kill. ('I'll stay till it stops raining . . . to miss the traffic . . . till the pub opens.')

Brings out an order form at every meeting's end

He conjures up an order form at the end of the meeting, like bringing down the final curtain in a theatre play. This is supposed to represent the 'close' that he's heard so much about. It is a sacred ritual always performed in the closing act. With form in hand, he abides by the last law of sales induction: he 'asks for the order'.

He gets an order: *get out and stay out.*

The noble characteristic of this type of salesman is that he doesn't try to sell (he doesn't really know how). He just keeps *hoping* that somebody will buy. He may muddle along in the short term, thanks only to the law of averages, but in the long term he's doomed. He just keeps changing jobs, drifting from one company to another.

Monotonous and mean with words

Possessed of a monotone

This type is oblivious to his impediment, and goes through life inflicting misery on his listeners.

Whether he's selling as his vocation, or simply trying to sell his ideas and thus himself in an *everyday* context, he is destined to alienate any audience. On the telephone, monotony is magnified even more. (*PS: what is he doing in selling, anyway?*)

Uses minimum of facial expressions

His face shows no warmth or sincerity; he rarely smiles. It never occurs to him; he sees work as a serious business. Given no telltale signs of emotion, the prospect never knows whether the salesman is on his wavelength, or whether he cares and understands about his (the prospect's) business.

This type might just as well be hanging in the Louvre.

Speaks almost from a script

For some uncanny reason, this type is usually guilty of aggravating the situation even further – by speaking almost from a scripted presentation. There's no getting inside the other person's mind to identify the *type* and to tailor his words accordingly. It's a script – delivered in that characterless voice. Could anything be worse?

He's done it so many times it follows a set pattern. If the prospect comes up with a question or possible objection that's not in the script – forget it. It's just edited out. There's no room for improvisation.

Often talks over the other person

Observing this happen is quite painful; and when you're on the receiving end, it really hurts. We see it often on TV chat shows (Terry Wogan is gradually breaking the habit) and in other interview situations, when one person just talks *over* the other's words. This completely wipes out what the first speaker is saying – and, more importantly, it's very *rude*.

We are all guilty occasionally of talking at the same time as somebody else – in an argument, for example, or if we're excited about something. That's acceptable.

But it is *not* acceptable in a business situation – when you're trying to sell something. You need to know exactly what the prospect is saying so that you can formulate a reply. This is quite apart from how your manners will be judged. But the prospect won't voice his disapproval (*his body language will, if you're attuned*); he probably just won't buy.

Treats all prospects as homogeneous

He makes no allowances for varying types of buyers. He thus fails to get on to the same wavelengths as the many different individuals he meets. He approaches them all in exactly the same way; he carries on delivering his scripted presentation and remains a loser.

This type wins only when the prospect sells himself *into the idea* of making a purchase. It may be the only way of getting rid of the salesman. On rare occasions, it can be just plain pity. Or the buyer may be his clone in terms of personality – he's boring, speaks with a monotone and has no empathy. Snap: *one sale*!

Whatever they do in life, people of this type will find it very difficult to get their message across effectively. In the persuasion business (which they should definitely not be in) they're reducing their chances of success dramatically. Like the buyer said earlier on: get out and stay out.

Over-familiar, over the top

Uses first name too soon

He calls the client by his first name as soon as contact is made (often on the phone).

This point needs to be sorted out. Say you're telephoning a new prospect for the very first time. The secretary puts you through to her boss, Nick Peters, and you say to this stranger: 'Hi Nick. It's Tom Smith from MBI speaking . . .' Such forwardness is rarely well received. Many prospects object to over-familiarity; they might accept it at the end of the call *after* speaking to you, but not while you're an unknown quantity. To many people it immediately spells insincerity. Whatever you say after that is lost.

The first-name approach is an accepted part of business practice in the USA. But here, English reserve still dictates a certain protocol. So start on a formal footing until you've established some kind of rapport.

The same rule applies to your first dealings with anybody at the client's office – particularly his secretary.

Flatters client insincerely

There's nothing wrong with the odd compliment or piece of flattery if it's meant sincerely. If appropriate, it can be taken as a positive show of interest and set a pleasant mood to a meeting.

Insincere flattery could have a much worse effect than labelling you as superficial. It could introduce doubt into the prospect's mind: 'If you can flatter me, *then you are probably also flattering the product you are trying to sell me*. So I don't trust you.'

Regards listening as time wasting: has to talk non-stop

This type goes on speaking without pausing for breath. He

believes that silence is a void that has to be filled – by *him*, not by the prospect. After all, he's selling; so he is required to do all the talking.

Unfortunately he's never listened long enough to learn the error of his ways. What hope!

Over-enthusiastic about benefits of his product

He refuses to believe or even consider that there are any possible negative points or flaws about the product he sells. He's so fixed by that common directive 'to be positive' (or the flip side – not to be negative) that he carries it too far. As far as he's concerned, what he's offering is simply the best. He won't encourage a dialogue that might get his prospects to *voice* their possible objections so that these can be laid to rest. He just doesn't give them a chance to weigh things up.

Shows visible sulk on rejection

When the prospect indicates a verdict of thumbs down, he sits there mortified. ('What? You've made me speak non-stop for the last 45 minutes for nothing; you cannot be serious!')

Instead of probing for the *reason* for no sale, he may aggravate the situation by telling the prospect that:

1   He drove two hours in the rain to get there.
2   Not buying is a big mistake.
3   The prices are going up in twenty minutes.

He has then ruined any chance of the door being left open for future contact (by him or anyone else from his company).

People can change their minds at a later date. It's natural. We all do. Circumstances change. The prospect may read some favourable editorial about your company; he may receive a bigger budget the following year; somebody may recommend your organization. Or you may have just caught him on a bad day the first time round.

If you've left the door open and parted amicably, then there may be another opportunity. He would probably be amenable to a further approach. But if you've challenged his decision and reacted badly to losing out on this occasion – then you've burned your boats.

This type of salesperson, if he does sell, rarely gets any repeat business from his customers. They're usually just one-off orders. He never establishes any degree of rapport with people generally, and business contacts in particular.

If somebody does buy and then becomes dissatisfied with some element, and complains to this salesperson, he faces the same inflexibility and insincerity that he first encountered (and initially excused).

The result: loss of goodwill. The company's image has been tarnished. When successive salespeople contact the *same* prospect (because this type has moved on to another unsuspecting employer) they are given a hostile reception. An individual's reputation has labelled the whole of the company that he represents or represented.

Confident: it's in your interest to buy from me

Acknowledges that client may be busy

This type sells himself from the first minute by recognizing that the prospect is a busy person, and communicating that fact.

Being inaccessible to all and sundry is equated with status. So when you acknowledge somebody has limited time, you're saying between the lines: 'I know you're in demand, therefore I appreciate you taking time to talk to me (but it's worth it – otherwise I wouldn't be bothering you).' The implication makes the prospect more amenable. He's a busy man in an important position which affords him esteem – the esteem of people *showing* that they appreciate being given some of his time.

There is further prestige – for both of you – in letting him know that *you* are busy too. He wants to deal with other busy/successful people – like you. It makes you members of the same club. So let him know your time is valuable by taking the cue for leaving, or tell him how much time *you* can spare.

Here the salesman is really *helping to shape the prospect's perception* of him. He then uses it to his advantage.

Lets prospect decide on discussion of pleasantries

In our first dealings with people we all need warming up, rather like an athlete preparing for a race. With the prospect, the aim is to try to establish a rapport early on. It can be awkward for both parties if you haven't met before; but it's a bit worse for you because you are the visitor while he's on home ground. You're the one who has to prove something.

So let the client take the lead. If you end up talking about something which he is interested enough to prolong, and he's enjoying the discussion, then fine. He's running the show. That's what you're there for anyway. To get inside his mind. To find out what makes him tick, what are his interests and his values. Everything follows from that. You know that from your own experiences.

You're selling yourself as a good listener. People like that; you're a rare breed (remember Chapter 4). Let him decide when to cut short.

Makes the client feel comfortable in his presence

This must be the most valuable quality of this type of salesperson. Most clients' attitudes and reactions will be shaped by your demeanour. If you are tense, you may make the other person so. If you smile, you'll probably find it's contagious.

You're trying to sell something – so you must first sell the *mood* that you want to prevail throughout your meeting.

You want him to be relaxed (because people give more of themselves when they feel this way), so be comfortable within yourself. Look as though you're bent on enjoying your meeting and want to help him. With a smile in the voice, you're letting him know that there is no compulsion at all, so he needn't be on his guard. You're showing him in an affable way that it's in his interest to buy this product – and that he has the added advantage of dealing with *you*.

The person you are seeing may be serious and might need drawing out. He may just be worried or in a bad mood. You have to do a persuasion job, so you want him in a receptive frame of mind. People will generally mirror your mood after a while. If you have a person sitting opposite you being pleasant, it's hard not to be pleasant back to them. Be patient. Try it.

Asks lots of questions and shows genuine interest

As already established, the key to getting inside the mind is well-targeted questioning. Your questions steer the prospect to talk about his needs, doubts, fears. You are then prepared to tailor your offer accordingly.

Asking questions means automatically becoming *involved* with the prospect's business. This helps to fade out the salesman image and give the impression of somebody who is there to help – an adviser. A show of genuine interest and concern for his business makes the prospect more inclined to be forthcoming. And the more snippets offered, the easier it becomes to read his mind and work out those *hidden* needs that people are often so reluctant to divulge.

Maintains eye contact most of the time

The point is often laboured. But successful negotiators in all walks of life will testify to the fact that the eyes can reveal all.

Watch the eyes next time you're talking to somebody. When you ask a question and you're given the answer, read the eye message too. We often say one thing and then provide a *supplementary* answer with the eyes. It can be a valuable way of finding out what somebody is *really* thinking. This successful type of salesman does pick up these signals.

Sincerity shows through the eyes – when people really feel strongly or really mean something. Similarly, if you're lying or being insincere the astute person can pick this up.

By maintaining eye contact you will look as though you are listening. This gives more depth to the conversation. *You* look interested – so his interest is sustained.

If you look somebody squarely in the eye it gives the impression that you're being 'up front'. It's worth mentioning that spectacle wearers can have a problem here. Light reflection on their lenses means that the person looking at them sees only rays of light. This is not very good for making and maintaining eye contact, and it can be off-putting for the onlooker. Lenses are now available with a coating which completely cuts out this light.

Heavily tinted or dark glasses are not to be recommended. They may be useful if you're on the run from Interpol, or selling from the back of a lorry with a half-lit cigarette drooping from the left side of your mouth. But they will certainly prevent eye messages being sent or picked up by the other party. You won't be able to *make* eye contact – let alone keep it.

Some salespeople carry eye contact too far. It becomes piercing, and the prospect feels uncomfortable. This is not conducive to getting what you're after. You don't want to force the other person to look away.

10

Negotiating to win

Problem: everybody wants to be the winner. Who wants to be the loser? There's no fun in losing. But what constitutes a win is normally *subjective*. It's in the mind – your mind. The game of negotiation differs from all other games. That's because with this, we're looking for *two* winners.

The process of negotiation starts only when the sale has been agreed – in principle. You've done the selling; the other person is convinced of the benefits and is in the right frame to buy – save for certain fine points.

What points? It could be anything. It can be trivial in reality, as far as you're concerned. But it's *significant* in the other buyer's mind. And *that's* what's significant.

Many people think that negotiation is always to do with price. Of course this is not so. Cost is not always the only sticking factor; it can be delivery, payment terms, packaging, added extras or after-sales service.

It's a joy to watch professionals negotiating – not necessarily the sale of a product, but any sale. Government ministers, for instance, negotiate every day all over the world; they trade concessions with other parties. It's exactly the same negotiating process, with both sides gaining something.

But most salespeople do not understand the reasoning

behind the principles of negotiation. They confuse the terms 'selling' and 'negotiating'. It's important to *differentiate* between the two. Remember, negotiation takes place after the sale. There are many who manage to sell but then fail to negotiate effectively and end up with no sale. You can see then that the consummate salesperson has to be master of the whole process.

But the plain truth is that the majority are poor negotiators. They can just about get by in convincing the prospect that he ought to buy, using the scripted arguments laid down as law at the sales induction course. Then – reality stares him in the face. The buyer wants certain concessions in order to tie up the deal. Now you have to be on your mettle. Forget the script – or forget the sale.

An understanding of the psychology behind negotiation can really improve results. Let's define the scenario:

1   You know that he or she wants a better deal (they have budgets, after all).
2   He or she knows that equally the salesperson wants a good deal (after all, you have margins).

Who budges?

No one can be blamed for asking for a better deal. There was never a truer maxim than: if you don't ask, you don't get. But just because the customer or prospect asks for something, it doesn't mean that you have to give it. If it's reasonable and it clinches the sale without too much aggravation, monetary sacrifice or bad feeling, then fine. But if *both* parties are not satisfied, then the equation is not right. Remember – it's a game with two winners.

If one half of the negotiating equation is not happy, then the situation is unsatisfactory because:

1   An unhappy customer is not likely to buy from you again (and may pick faults with your product or service after delivery – and possibly withhold payment).

2   Equally, an unhappy salesman is unlikely to give good
    service *during* and *after* the sale. The customer wanted
    the concession, but *not* at the expense of something else.
    That wasn't part of the deal.

Since negotiating is essentially a trading of *concessions*, we're
looking for *amicable* compromise. We've brought the prospect on to the buying plane, and the mood should not turn
now.

Fact: with increasing competition and better market
awareness, most selling today requires some element of
negotiation before a deal is finalized. Very few transactions
are: 'Yes – I'll take it.'

Fact: subconsciously, most buyers are not really after
better price, delivery or payment terms. They just don't like
being *sold* to; they'd much prefer to *buy* (i.e when the control
is with them). Therefore, if they win concessions from the
salesperson (on price or whatever) they feel they have bought
rather than been sold to (ego). In effect there's been a *reversal*
of roles; they've 'sold' to the salesperson (so the customer
feels he's the winner). Now there's a switch!

So let the customer feel he has bought; this is the key to
successful selling. It's based on the weaknesses of human
nature. You're selling to a person, remember? Not to bricks
and mortar.

Have certain concessions *up your sleeve* which, if need be,
you can bring into play. And perhaps a major concession
which you can be flexible about. But don't offer them all
immediately; *leave something in the hat after the rabbit's
been pulled out*.

Game plan

Salesman's problem: I don't know what your *bottom line* is. I
don't know how much you are willing to spend, or what
you'll settle for ultimately. So I want you to make the first
move.

Customer's problem: I don't know how *far* I can push you on price, delivery or payment. So we'll play ping-pong until someone digs in his heels and refuses to budge. If that's me, *you* make the concession.

You're treading a thin tightrope all the time. If your original demand is too high, then you turn off the buyer and you don't even get to the negotiation stage.

And yet you've got to give yourself room enough to manoeuvre. If you give *your* bottom line figure immediately with no concessions (because you've already included your concessions in the 'package') then the prospect doesn't feel *he was ever in the match*. He gets no feeling of having come out with a trophy above his head; he hasn't won.

If you watch experienced negotiators at work, whether it be arms control, wage tribunals, economic summits or in the boardroom, you will see the dependence on body and facial reactions. You'll see as much language coming from the body as the mouth.

It's tough psychologically because you don't want to alienate the other person. After all, he's in the right frame of mind for buying; it's just these concessions that he's seeking. If you watch the pros you see how they let the body signal their response to a demand. You'll see them shaking their head, smiling, flicking an imaginary speck of fluff off their tie or jacket or occasional outbursts of laughter in disbelief.

They're trying to let the other person know, without saying 'You need your head tested', that the request is over the top. It's less offensive using body language. The other person doesn't know whether what he's asked for is fair, anyway, and is being given the signal that his reasoning is wrong. The prospect may not have expected such a big concession anyway – but he needs to know how *close* he can get to it.

Concessions

The trading of concessions highlighted here, which takes

place in any negotiating situation, is marked by the fact that they're often just *subjective* in the negotiator's mind.

Getting inside the other person's mind is crucial here, as the ego demands of the buyer have to be met. If you can work out in what area his principal needs and fears lie, it will help you to decide which *bait* you need to use and how far you have to spread the net. Take some examples:

1 Is he worried about the fact that your envelopes are not as burst resistant as those of his present suppliers? You could offer to pay for postage and cost of contents and envelope for any packages returned by the postal authorities. This is a small concession for you, but *big* in his mind. *Sale clinched*.

2 Is he worried because he'd have to dip into a reserve budget to pay for the whole amount, because his new budget operates in five weeks time? You could offer to invoice at the beginning of his new budgetary period. This is a small concession for you, but *big* for him. *Sale clinched*.

3 Is he worried that a delivery let-down could lose him his own important contract? You could offer to send goods by overnight air freight at your expense if you have a problem on your side. This would save eight days. He buys peace of mind from you: a small concession for you, a *big* one for him. *Sale clinched*.

Generally, of course, you'll be pushed (or only allow yourself to be pushed) up to the limit of what concessions you're able to authorize during a meeting. The buyer can usually sense this from your own hesitance and body signals. If that's not enough and he wants to go further, then you may have to consult with somebody. This can have an advantage and a disadvantage.

The advantage is that you are out of deadlock and have breathing space to check and see if there's anything else you can offer that can ease the situation. And of course you can actually consult with other relevant people to see if you can go further (that's if you want to). Also the buyer thinks you're considering him seriously as a customer and are actually working behind the scenes to sort things out. But beware of leaving things too long; a competitor can come in on the scene.

The disadvantage is that you've perhaps worked hard at building up momentum towards a deal during your visit(s) and interest is running high (remember the attention curve). It's just these concessions that have so far prevented the deal being concluded.

Now you go away. This can change things. The buyer *doesn't have a particularly good memory; he forgets all the benefits that he was so excited about at the previous meeting.* It's natural. So many things have happened since then: his roof fell in; his company lost a big contract; his budgerigar has gone missing; he's fallen out with his boss. In short, you've been overtaken by events. His interest is not running so high. That's natural. He probably needs to be resold – but he's too busy to see you now.

Or, as quite often happens, he's had time to shop around and has achieved a satisfactory deal more quickly elsewhere. ('But why didn't he tell me he was also talking to someone else?' He did. Remember? But you thought he was bluffing.) His boss was pressing him to make the purchasing decision fast – so he went ahead once satisfied. Also the rival salesman had full authority to agree to the deal *there and then.* A missed opportunity.

Timing is so important in selling; let no one forget it.

Concluding

If you want to avoid reaching stalemate and having to leave the meeting to check on something (because you feel there is a danger of the prospect going cold, as seen in the previous example), you should end the ritual. Produce the ace up your sleeve.

'OK then. If we get the stock to you already packaged with your logo printed, and we do it within three weeks – *at no extra charge* – is that a deal?'
    'You're on.'

You should emulate a lawyer summing up at the end of a courtroom hearing at this final stage. What you do is to *restate* what you're actually giving.

During this *inner game of selling*, people get so obsessed with the play in progress that they forget what they've actually asked for!! Analysis: by restating what you have now conceded to the client, you are psychologically affirming what a good deal *he* has managed to get out of you. Game, set and match to him!

    Or is it to you both?!!

11

Making words work for you

Do you overlook the power of words in the selling situation? Are you aware how some words seem to work and others don't? Do you choose your words carefully and monitor their effect? The subtleties of making word associations work for you are not discussed often enough in the context of selling.

Think about it. You want to convey something to somebody. You have in your mind an image which you *translate* into words. The other person takes your words and translates them *back* into an image – but his *own* image. What if it doesn't correspond to the image that you are trying to put over? Communication has not been effective. The word associations that were sparked off by your choice of words may have produced a negative result.

Consider this example. A personnel manager is standing in the corridor with the managing director. He says to a passing secretary:

'Have you seen Tom Collins? We need to discuss the training budget.'

'Yes – as a matter of fact I saw him about ten minutes ago, tottering up the stairs towards accounts.'

It's 2.30, so the PM assumes Collins has been for a liquid lunch. His mind has latched on to the word 'tottering', with all its implications. He now has a mental image of Collins being below par, and doesn't want to risk the MD seeing him in this state. He makes an excuse for deferring the meeting.

In actual fact:

1   The secretary had just used the word 'tottering' because it was the first one to come into her head. She had actually meant to say 'trotting' but it came out as 'tottering'.
2   Collins had been weightlifting during his lunch break, or playing squash (so he looked and felt tired).
3   He was suffering from a bad attack of migraine.

But the use of that one throwaway word had introduced a *negative* association into his boss's mind. The personnel manager's conception of Collins was now that of someone who drinks too much at lunch time. It was wrong. But the idea had taken root. An assumption brands somebody as a drunkard when he is not. (Dean Martin has the same problem!) A single word and its connotation have caused the problem.

Is it any wonder that psychologists are now conducting extensive research into how words affect our minds and emotions? They've dubbed this *psycholinguistics*.

Of course, with human nature being so complex, it's impossible to know exactly how particular words will be interpreted and thus received. But if we can get inside the mind of the individual, we can usually work out which type of person we are dealing with. Then we can choose the words which have the best chance of having the desired effect.

Take an example. A sales manager is annoyed at the unusually poor quality of his secretary's typing. The number of serious mistakes is becoming intolerable.

'Sandra – your typing's very shoddy lately. It's important that the invoices go out accurately. It's bad enough as it is with sales being down.'

The instant Sandra hears the word 'shoddy', her blood pressure rises and she becomes defensive. She's bitter at the personal affront. Doesn't he know, she thinks, that those two extra people transferred from head office are giving me lots of work? I'm snowed under. How am I supposed to cope? Doesn't he consider that? He can keep his invoices. He can keep his job! Exit.

The sales manager would probably still have had Sandra on his payroll if his approach had been:

'Sandra – your typing's not up to its usual impressive standard. Any problems?'

This is now an invitation for her to offer reasons. After all, she wants to justify not reaching her normal *impressive standard*.

'Well, Mr Keen, I'm sorry about that. The truth is, I just can't cope. Those two extra marketing people from head office give me at least eight letters a day each.'

'Oh, I didn't realize. Sales are down, as you know, and if invoices go out with errors it holds up payment. OK, I'll see if I can get their typing done by Mrs . . .'

Net result: he's had a chance to compliment *and* criticize (nicely), and Sandra now strives to reach her former impressive standard again. Oh – and he still has a secretary!

Studying how words affect our minds and emotions is fascinating because we are constantly in communication with people. Not just in a business context, but also in everyday situations. We give and receive words all the time – when we are reading, writing, listening and speaking. Surely a moment's thought as to how a word or phrase could be interpreted by another person is worth the effort? Use of the wrong choice of word has precipitated many divorces, wars, fights, and business bust-ups.

As we are all practitioners of persuasion, our basic tools are words. But like all good craftsmen we have to know which are the right ones to select from the toolkit for the job in hand. It's usually laziness that prevents people from doing this. Of course, it's easier to just leave the brain in the low gears and say to the other person:

'I disagree totally with what you're saying.'

'I'm not happy with your work.'

'I'm afraid we can't deliver for eight weeks.'

'I regret to inform you . . .'

'I know you think our reputation is dubious . . .'

'You must tell me how much you're paying at the moment if I'm to . . .'

People spend their time brainwashing others that things are *worse* than they really are. Why do they do it? They're making it hard for themselves by creating a bad feeling where there needn't have been one. Get inside the mind.

There are much better ways of phrasing the preceding statements. How about:

'Won't you look at it this way instead?'

'Any reason why your sales figures have slipped?'

'We'll get the goods to you within eight weeks.'

'We have to tell you . . .'

'Our reputation has been enhanced since . . .'

'It would be helpful if I knew how much . . .'

If only people bothered to think about the effect of their words when trying to sell a product, solve a complaint, get a date, make an apology, defend themselves to their boss, or get past a secretary. It's highly likely the results would be favourable.

If you've ever played the word association game, you'll know how your mind triggers off an image in the subconscious. It's quite automatic. A word evokes a certain feeling and a picture in the mind.

So in any selling situation, make sure that the message being communicated is said in the right words at the right time. You are far more likely to get the result you are after. We're talking not about *deception* but about *perception*: using the right tools for the right job, understanding the psycholinguistic connotations of saying things in a certain way.

A true story

The marketing manager of a company wanted to attend a six-day conference in Las Vegas. The conference fee and travel expenses would add up to quite an expensive trip. His boss was the type who didn't like spending the company's money. If he authorized any outlay, he would always want to see an immediate return. Furthermore, if people went on overseas trips, it had to be work, work, work all the way.

The marketing manager, Mr X, knew that the month of July (when the conference was being held) was a fairly slack time for the company and for himself. So the timing was good. He could probably overcome the cost objection by telling his boss that many of his counterparts in rival companies would be there.

But he feared that one thing would kill it stone dead. The idea of Las Vegas. It was bound to conjure up a totally unsuitable image in the mind of his boss: *gambling, Caesar's Palace, scantily clad showgirls* – everything except a serious conference. It wasn't contrived. Las Vegas just happened to be the venue, although obviously that was part of the attraction of going. So Mr X decided that when he went to sell the conference to his boss, he would draw attention to the covenient date and would mention the country (USA) rather than the specific venue.

This is how the meeting went:

'Come in. Sit down.'

'Thanks. I'll get to the point quickly. I was wondering. July is quite slack here, and the ADM conference takes place then – in America. I'd like to go. It would be useful for us to have representation there. All the competition are going.'

'Mm . . . how much?'

'Well. Delegate fee plus travel . . . suppose about £3000– 3500.'

'That's quite expensive. You know we're over on the T&E budget already.'

'Yes, I know. But I really feel this would be a good year to attend. There's a two day seminar on . . .'

'Hey, I've got an idea. If you could use the parent company's apartment on Manhattan east side, that would cut down on accommodation costs.'

'Oh – but that's in New York.'

'Well – that's where the conference is, isn't it? That's what you said.'

'No I didn't.'

(Interesting – how word association is at work *already* Don only mentioned America, but his boss assumed it was New York, and also accused him of having said so!)

'Well, where is it being held?'

Mr X thought he was cornered; it looked as though his cause was lost. Then he had a brainwave; he used a psycho-linguistic trick.

'Where is it. Oh – Nevada.'

'Nevada. Oh . . . yes, Nevada.' (Pause) 'Er . . . do they have an airport there?'

'Oh yes. And domestic flights are cheap too.'

'Well.' (Pause) 'OK, but keep the costs down.'

A happy ending.

Look at what happened, and the thinking behind the persuader's moves:

1   The marketing manager had anticipated the association that Las Vegas would conjure up in his boss's mind.
2   So he decided to mention just the United States.
3   He came unstuck because his boss had *imagined* he'd said New York (people have poor memories – remember!!).
4   He had to say where it was now. So he said Nevada. It was the truth. It was in Nevada.

This was perfectly all right. It was up to his boss if he wanted to know *more*. But the point is, he probably would not have been booking a plane ticket if he had mentioned Las Vegas. He had to get inside the mind of his boss and anticipate his interpretation of certain ideas. Having got over this hurdle, he then emphasized that domestic flights were cheap. That struck the final chord.

So back to basics. Psychologists have given word associations the label of 'psycholinguistics'. But what we're talking about is something that we should be aware of every day: how words affect our responses; selective use of words; *tactful use of words to get the desired results*. In the example you could say that the man with a motive *helped* his boss to make an objective decision. As already stated: we all need to be persuaded to take a course of action. We're looking for good reasons to do something. We want the other person to convince us of why we should do something. It's their skilful use of words that tips the balance.

You have to use words to communicate. You may as well choose the best.

12

Acting the part – wrongly and rightly

This chapter follows the fortunes of a sales manager. The first shows how not to do it. The second demonstrates the art of successful selling.

Dealing with the secretary

Wrong

'Putting you through now.'
   'Mr Saxby's office.'
   'Hello. I'd like to talk to Mr Saxby.'
   'Who's calling him?'
   'It's Humphrey Blake, Corrugated Casings Ltd.'
   'May I ask what it's to do with?'
   'It's something I'd like to discuss with him.'
   'Has he spoken to you before, Mr Blake?'
   'No – he hasn't.'
   'Just a moment.'
   'I've just had a word with Mr Saxby. Could you tell me what it's about?'
   'Well, OK then. We sell corrugated packaging and I wanted to come and see him.'

'One moment.'

'I've had another word with him. He's in a meeting at the moment. He's rather tied up. He said if you'd like to write in he'll get in touch if he's interested.'

'No, you don't understand. I have to speak to him. I can't put it in the post.'

'I'm sorry but he's very busy.'

'So am I!' (Click)

Right

'Could you give me the name of Mr Saxby's secretary, please?'

'Yes – it's Pauline Sims.'

'Would you put me through to her?'

'Putting you through.'

'Mr Saxby's office.'

'Yes, hello. Could I speak to Pauline Sims please?'

'Speaking.'

'Miss Sims – good morning. Can you help me? The names's Blake.' (Pause) 'My company is Corrugated Casings. I'd like a quick word with Mr Saxby if he's available now.'

'Well I know he's rather tied up at the moment. I'll see. Does he know what it's concerning?'

'He probably knows my company. Would you tell him it's about a new range that I think he'd want to hear about? If he's busy now, perhaps you could ask him when I might have a few words with him.'

'Just a second, Mr Blake. Would you mind holding?'

'No – take your time, Miss Sims.'

'Mr Blake. He said he'll be free in around half an hour. If you leave your number he'll call you back.'

'No, that's OK. I'll call back in about forty-five minutes.'

'Very well.'

'Thanks for your help. Bye.'

After forty-five minutes:

'Mr Saxby's office.'
  'Is Pauline Sims there?'
  'Speaking – is that Mr Blake?'
  'Yes. Hello again.'

  'Putting you through now.' (Click)
  'Bill Saxby speaking.'

Securing an appointment

Wrong

He replaced the receiver and almost simultaneously picked it up again, flicking through his personal organizer file with his other hand. He dialled again.

  'Good morning. HYK Pneumatics. How can I help you?'
  'Morning. Could you tell me who the office supplies manager is?'
  'I'm not sure – I'm a temp here. I'll see if I can find out . . . just a moment, I have another call . . . right, office supplies. Let me see. Could you hold on a minute?'
  'Yes.'

Three minutes of piped music later:

'I've been through to customer service. They said it depends.'
  'Depends on what?'
  'I'm not sure.'
  'Look – just put me through to them please.'
  'Hold on.'

Two minutes later:

'I've spoken to them again. They said were you selling something.'

'Well, as it happens I am.'

'In that case it's Mr Sheppard. I'll connect you to his secretary. I'm not sure whether she's in yet.' (Click)

'Sheppard speaking.' (Hurried and impatient voice)

'Ah, Mr Sheppard. I'm through to you. That's great. Humphrey Blake of Corrugated Casings Ltd speaking. I've got some new packaging that's the best in its field. We've had lots of interest from the trade press. I'd like to come and see you. Now would Tuesday at 9.15 suit you, or Thursday at 2.30?'

'Just a moment, Mr Corrigan.' The prospect is heard speaking in the background to somebody who is obviously with him in his office. 'Now what was that?'

'Er – I was saying. Would Tuesday at 9.15 be OK, or would you prefer Thursday at 2.30?'

'Well – neither really.'

'Sorry – what do you mean?'

'Well, Mr Corrigan – what is it exactly you wanted to talk to me about?'

'As I said. A new line we've got.'

'What's the name of your company again, Mr Corrigan?'

'It's Corrugated Casings. Actually my name's Blake – Humphrey Blake.'

'Right. Sorry, Mr Blake. I'm in the middle of a meeting right now. My secretary's not in yet. Give me your number.'

'My number – er – it's 768 0077.'

'I'll call you back in fifteen minutes. Goodbye, Mr Case.'

Two hours later, and no call.

Right

'Good morning. HYK Pneumatics. How can I help you?'

'Morning. You *could* help me by telling me who the manager of your office supplies department is.'

'I'll just check for you sir. Could you hold for a moment?'

'Certainly. Thank you.'

'I've spoken to customer services. They said it depends on what it's to do with.'

'Right. I understand. Could you put me through to them please?'

'Yes. Who shall I say is calling?'

'My name's Blake.'

'Trying to connect you, Mr Blake.'

'Customer services. Jill Court speaking. Is that Mr Blake?'

'Yes. Good morning. I just need to know who's now responsible for purchase of office supplies.'

'Certainly. That's David Sheppard. Is there anything I could help you with?'

'Well – I'd like to have a brief word with Mr Sheppard, if he's available, about a range of products my company's just launched. I think he'd want to know about it.'

'Would you like me to put you through to his secretary?'

'That would be good, Mrs Court. Thank you.'

'Let me see if she's there.' (Click) 'Mr Blake, she doesn't seem to be answering. I'll put you through directly to Mr Sheppard's extension.'

'Sheppard speaking.'

'Mr Sheppard. Mrs Court has just transferred me to you. The company's Corrugated Casings.' (Pause) 'My name's Blake. Is it convenient to talk?'

'Well – actually I'm with somebody at the moment. But go ahead. What's it about?'

'Oh – I've called at an inconvenient time. Can I call you later, when you're free? I'd rather do that.'

'Very well. I should be free at around 11.30.'

'OK. I'll call you then.'

'Sorry, what was your name again?'

'The company's Corrugated Casings. My name's Blake.'

'Right. I'll speak to you later, Mr Blake.'

'Bye.'

At 11.35 a.m.:

'Mr Sheppard. It's Humphrey Blake here. I called you an hour ago.'

'Yes, Mr Blake. Corrugated Casings, isn't it? What can I do for you?'

'Well, we have a new range called Tyne X which I believe you would be interested to hear about. I'd like to fix up a brief meeting with you.'

'When would you like to come? I'm up to my eyes in it this week.'

'Well, to be specific, I wondered whether there might be a chance of say Tuesday at around 9.15. Or if that's awkward, Thursday at around 2.30.'

'Thursday would be better. 2.30 did you say?'

'Yes. Can we make it between 2.30 and 2.45, just in case I have parking problems?'

'Yes, that's OK. I should be clear most of that afternoon, so that would be fine.'

'Thank you. See you then.'

'Goodbye, Mr Blake.'

The first meeting

Wrong

Reflecting on his unsuccessful telephone encounters, Blake left his office for the first of three meetings he had fixed for the day.

To receptionist: 'Morning. I've an appointment with Mr Banks for 11.45.'

'Your name sir?'

'Humphrey Blake. Corrugated Casings.'

'Would you take a seat.'

After a time, he is led to the prospect's office.

'Good morning, Mr Banks.'

    'Good morning, Mr . . . er Mr . . .'

'Blake.'

'Yes. Sorry to keep you waiting out there.'

'That's OK' as he sits down. 'It's a pleasure to meet you. It's good of you to see me, especially after the last fiasco. I can't apologise enough. Must be a year ago now, I suppose. Hope your company didn't lose that important contract.'

    'Now what fiasco was that, Mr Blake?'

'Oh – you know. I dealt with your predecessor, Mr Flint. You got the wrong consignment from us. A mess-up in Finland. Still, all's well that ends well. I managed to get the lead time reduced from five weeks to four weeks for your replacements.'

    'I see.' Puzzled look. The prospect's mind is distracted now. He's intrigued to discover more about the previous dealings with Mr Blake.

'Now, Mr Banks. I wanted to discuss this new line called Tyne X. It's similar to the standard DY range.'

    'How much is it?'

'Well – it's £6.40 per unit, with bulk discounts after 200.'

    'That's expensive.'

'Yes, but it's a superior range. I've got some testimonials I can show you.' He reaches for his case and rummages around for several minutes.

    In the meantime the prospect decides to make a call. 'John – hello, it's Greg here. I have a gentleman from Corrugated Casings with me . . . Yes. That's right. Oh . . . sure, I understand. Yes. £6.40. Oh, did they? Bye for now.'

'Here, I've found one of the testimonials.'

    The prospect glances at the piece of paper but is clearly detached from the proceedings. 'How do the bulk discount figures work? Is it done on a quarterly basis?'

'Well, it depends on how high you go quantity-wise. For example . . .' Out comes his calculator.

Mr Banks's attention is drawn back to the pile of files on his desk and the problem of getting through them. He's now anxious to make a start.

'Let me give you this sheet here. I've scribbled down the various discounts and payment periods.'

'Thank you, Mr Blake. Now, if you'll excuse me I've got some pressing work to get on with. Thank you for coming to see me.'

'No – it's my pleasure. As I said, it's great to make contact again after the last foul-up. Shall I give you a call in about two days or so?'

'No, don't bother. I mean – I'll get in touch with you if I'm interested.'

'Bye for now.'

Mr Banks is left thinking: 'I'm certainly not using that company. They may let us down again. That wouldn't go down well with the boss. Anyway, at that price, who needs to take a chance? As a new boy I'm still in the probation period. What a waste of time that was.'

As Humphrey Blake started up his car, he thought to himself: 'That went well. I'm sure that won't turn out to be a waste of time!'

Right

'Good morning.' He hands over his business card to the receptionist. 'I've an appointment with Mr Banks at 11.45.'

'Would you take a seat.' The receptionist walks away with his business card and returns shortly to accompany him to the prospect's office.

'Good morning, Mr Banks.'

'Good morning, Mr Blake. Do sit down.'

Banks studies the business card. 'I see your office is in the City. Have you come from there now?'

'Yes I have.'

'The traffic's a nightmare around there now. Not a pleasant journey, I would have thought.'

'Well – it wasn't too bad this morning. Still, can't complain.'

'Yes. Has its advantages being there. You're in the thick of it. Close to everything. Right. What have you got for me?'

'I wanted to talk to you about our new range called Tyne X. I've got something here that explains a bit about it. Are you still using these products?'

'Oh yes. We use one of your competitors, as I'm sure you're already aware. I've only been here three months now, but I'm putting new budgets together and I've budgeted for an increase in quantity.'

'I see.'

'How much do you charge per unit?'

'Well – the unit rates vary according to quantity and credit terms. Can I ask you – what quantity do you consume in a year, for example?'

'I have a printout here somewhere. Mmmm – looks like around 4000 units a year.'

'Is that likely to increase or remain stable? You mentioned that you had budgeted for an increase in quantity. Is that on the cards?'

'Oh yes. We're shipping more and more overseas. So we certainly will increase the quantity. Tell me. Do any other companies in our line of business use this new range?'

'Yes. I've got an article here about one of our customers and it mentions our product.' He produces it instantly from a file.

After Banks has finished reading, he asks: 'How much are we talking about per unit then?'

'We've got bulk discounts, but the basic unit price you can work on is £6.40.'

'How much would the rate be for an initial order of say 150? I'd like to try it out.'

'Well the discounts start at 200 units. The rate drops to £5.10.'

'What about over 200 units? What's the rate then?'

'Well from 300 to 400 it's £4.70, and from 401 to 600 it's £4.30.'

The prospect has a calculator on his desk and begins to work out some figures. Simultaneously, Blake begins to work out some calculations.

'What quantity are you looking at, Mr Banks?'

'Well I'm just working out what 500 would be as a starter.'

'I make that £2150. Do you agree?'

'Yes. Does that include VAT and delivery, Mr Blake?'

'It includes VAT, Mr Banks. I'm sure we can waive the despatch costs on this occasion, since you're trying us out.'

'OK. I'll go for that.'

'Good. I'll get that organized.'

'But Mr Blake. There's a condition. I need them quickly if we're to go ahead.'

'If you can just sign this agreement form now, we'll get them to you within three weeks.'

'Three weeks. OK. If there's a chance of sooner, I'd appreciate it. Now I'd better sign this agreement of yours.'

The second meeting

Wrong

'Mr Peters will be with you in a moment. Perhaps you'd like to go on into his office and wait, Mr Blake.'

'Thank you.'

Blake surveyed the large office: an imposing circular table with three chairs (with two half-full cups of coffee on the table, a phone and a clean ashtray), numerous bookcases, and at the far corner a large mahogany desk covered in papers. A large plaque that adorned the wall caught his eye: 'L. Peters. Chairman of Campaign for Clear Air 1988'. He walked over to the desk, put down his oversize case and sat in the chair opposite it, removing a pair of gloves which were perched on the chair.

After a few minutes, since the prospect hadn't arrived, Blake walked over to the table, removed the ashtray and went back to his seat and lit a cigarette, putting the ashtray on the side of the desk.

Two minutes later: 'Ah – Mr Blake. Apologies. I just had to get these letters. My secretary's off sick today.'

He casts a sideways glance towards the circular table by the door and then walks over to Blake, shakes his out-stretched hand, notices the cigarette in the ashtray and pointedly walks towards the window and opens it. He then takes his seat at the desk.

'Er . . . can I remove this? Have you finished?' he says to Blake, pointing at the ashtray.

'Oh yes – of course.'

'Now, Mr Blake. It's about three weeks since you called me. Tell me again about what you'd like to discuss. I'll just sign these letters while you're talking.'

'Yes. Certainly. It's about our new range, Tyne X. I think it's just right for you. Have you read about it?'

Silence, as Peters is studying and signing various letters.

'Sorry – I said have you, er . . . read about it?'

Eventually when the prospect looks up: 'I missed that. Have I read what?'

'I was saying – have you read about our new range, Tyne X?'

'No, I can't say that I have.' He gets up, walks over to an out-tray, puts the letters in there and then returns to his desk.

Blake proffers a sheet of paper.

'How much is it?'

'I'm afraid it's not cheap. It works out at £1.30 per unit. But it's much more attractive than other competitive models.'

'Mmm – that's not cheap, is it?'

'No – but with raw materials in the Far East going up all the time, I would think that the cost will go up even further in the next two months. It's the time to buy.'

'Well, I'm only paying £1.05 a unit with our current suppliers. I can't see much difference in the product. We've had tremendous budget cuts. I don't think I could justify switching at that price. You're certainly not cheap.'

A knock on the door. 'Excuse me, Mr Peters. Could you sign this petty cash voucher for the milk? Mr Mollett is in Cambridge today.'

'Let's have a look at this, Sarah. What's this – £3.42, is it? I presume you've checked it's right, have you? Er . . . can somebody else not sign it?'

'There's nobody around, Mr Peters.'

'Oh – very well.' Glancing at Blake. '*Signing my life away again.*'

After the woman leaves: 'Now where were we?'

'Oh – let me think. Yes. You were saying that we weren't cheap.'

'Yes, of course. Why should we switch over to your company?'

Blake takes out a heavy catalogue from his case and places it *on the desk*, covering a number of sheets of paper. He takes out a looseleaf sheet and passes it over to Mr Peters.

'You see this one here – it comes in a number of sizes. You can order it in . . .'

Mr Peters is concerned at the heavy catalogue on his desk, which is covering what were once pristine pieces of paper. He keeps checking out of the corner of his eye that they're not being mutilated. ('Should I ask him to move that heavy thing? No – I suppose I was blunt enough about the cigarette.') This is a great distraction for him. Concentration has gone.

'Sorry, Mr Blake. What was that? What dimensions did you say?'

'I said that there were three main types. There – you see.

They're listed at the bottom of the page.'

'Yes, OK. I've got it now.'

The telephone rings and the prospect answers it. 'Yes. OK, Richard. I'll hold on while you look for it.'

Blake is staring directly at Peters and is showing, through the vernacular of the body, his impatience. The prospect, sensing this, asks him to carry on talking and puts his hand over the mouthpiece.

Blake continues: 'So you see. You can get a wider choice of product than you've had before. And we have an easy payment plan that is very attractive and will help your . . .'

Peters waves at Blake to stop talking as he resumes the phone conversation. 'Yes. That's fine, Richard. We'll pick up on that later. Bye for now.'

'I was going to say, Mr Peters, that this will help your cash flow.'

'Right. This is the easy payment plan you mentioned, isn't it? Look – what's the minimum order under this plan?'

'Well – 500 units.'

Peters taps a few keys of his calculator. 'So the payments would be as indicated here in this booklet. Is that right?'

'Yes. That's it.'

'I think we'll go for that.'

Blake produces an order form from his case with deft precision and places it in front of the prospect's nose. It's rather a *complicated* form with lots of technical details and the legendary small print. 'Perhaps you could just sign there and insert 500 in that box there right under that column "easy payment plan".'

Peters studies the form intensely and flicks over the page, glancing at the various columns. He looks perplexed. 'What does that mean, Mr Blake?'

'Oh, – don't worry about that. The form's a bit out of date. That doesn't apply to you anyway.'

'Look – the best thing, Mr Blake, is to leave this with me. I'll sort it out later after I've looked through it. I'll get it off to you in the post. Now what address is it? Did you give me a card earlier on?'

'No, I didn't. Here's my card . . . But is there a problem? Something you're unhappy about?'

'No – I'd just like to look through it before I sign it. I really haven't got time now.' Glances at Blake's card. 'Oh, you're based in Swinsworth. Tell me – is that old village bar still there? Chap with a patch over his eye used to run it.'

'You know that area, do you?'

'Yes – my wife comes from there. Anyway, must dash now. Thank you for coming, Mr Blake. I'll be in touch. Goodbye.'

'Er – yes – bye, Mr Peters.'

Two days later Mr Peters discovers the order form in his in-tray, glances through it carefully, and then asks his secretary to file it for the moment. Humphrey Blake is told a week later (when chasing up the order by telephone), by Mr Peters's secretary, that for the time being the order has been put on ice.

Humphrey Blake had been skating on thin ice.

Right

Blake walked into the office. The large desk by the window was full of papers. The circular table looked a better bet. His prospect obviously used this area, as there were two half-empty cups left there. He sat down at the table. From his case he removed some papers.

'Mr Blake – apologies. I just had to get these letters off today. My secretary's sick.' Handshake. Mr Peters sits down at the table.

'Mr Blake – it's three weeks since you telephoned me to arrange this meeting. Now remind me of what it's all about. If you don't mind I'll just sign these letters while you're talking.'

'No – that's OK. You sign them. I'll just get together some literature that I'd like to show you.'

Blake finishes shuffling his papers when he sees Mr Peters returning to the table after having deposited his letters in a tray.

'Right.' Blake hands over his business card; the other man reciprocates.

'Mm . . .' Peters is studying the Blake's business card. 'I didn't know your company was part of the Westfields Corporation.'

'Oh yes. They bought us in eighty-four.'

'Do you know a chap called Scott Fisher?'

'Yes – he's our sales director in Paris.'

'Is that so? I worked with him about twenty-five years ago in Florence. If you're talking to him, say "hello" from me.'

'Certainly. Now – I wanted to make you aware of this new range of ours called Tyne X. It would be helpful if you could give me an idea as to how you package the goods that you despatch.'

'Sure. We use a few companies. It's better that way. And these are the ones we use at the moment.' He produces some paper from a nearby cabinet and hands it to Blake, who puts it down in the middle of the table. He points to various illustrations and asks a number of questions.

'Now this is our new range.'

'What price are we talking about?'

 'Well, that is dependent on a number of things. I'd like to get an idea of the kind of products you're shipping.'

'Basically everything in this booklet. Have a look.'

'I see . . . Now we've got a range especially for what you in your booklet refer to as product codes CF2, FD6, JK8. And there's a generous easy payment plan that could enable you to stagger your requirements without losing the advantage of the bulk discount rate. Also there's a chance . . .'

A knock on the door. 'Excuse me, Mr Peters. Could you sign this petty cash voucher for the milk? Mr Mollett is in Cambridge today.'

'Let's have a look at this, Sarah. What's this – £3.42, is it? I presume you've checked it's right. Have you a pen? Look . . . er . . . are you sure there's nobody else who could sign it?'

'Nobody else is here, Mr Peters.'

'Oh – very well.' Turning his gaze to Blake. 'Signing my life away again.'

'Now where were we?'

'I'll just *recap*. I was saying that we have a range that would suit perfectly what you refer to in your booklet here as CF2, FD6, JK8.' Pointing. 'And there are easy payment plans – with no loss of bulk discount – if you wanted to stagger your requirements. Let me just show you in our folder here what would be suitable.'

Blake ceases talking while Peters studies the literature.

'Mmmm . . . it seems very good. How much is that range?'

'Well at the moment it's £1.30 per unit. But I hear that because of the situation in the Far East our raw material costs may be shooting up soon, so I would imagine that would cause prices to rise. But of course that will affect not only us but all the other companies in the industry.'

'I see. So you're saying £1.30 per unit. I'm only paying £1.05 per unit at the moment, on average. If I ordered the annual requirement from you now, for example, would I be protected from any price increases during the year?' Blake nods. '£1.30 – you're not cheap.'

Telephone interruption.

'Sorry – what was I saying?'

'You were saying that you'd want the price frozen for a year if you ordered the yearly requirement now. Well – I can tell you, I'll do that for you. D'you want to go ahead?'

'So what would 3000 units be? It's this column here in the payment chart – is that right? £3860 including the discount?'

'Yes. Shall we go ahead on that basis?'

'What's the delivery situation?'

'Between two and four weeks – or sooner if it's possible.'

'OK – I'll go ahead on that basis then.'

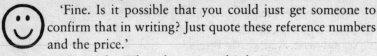

'Fine. Is it possible that you could just get someone to confirm that in writing? Just quote these reference numbers and the price.'

'Certainly. When do you need it by?'

'Your secretary's off sick today, isn't she? But if someone else could do it now, I'd be grateful. I need it to reserve your stock and hold the prices as agreed.'

'Very well. I'll get someone to issue a purchase requisition now, and you can take it with you.'

'That's good. I'll be sending you our standard form to sign in the next few days. It's just our internal form confirming your order.'

'That'll be fine. If you'd like to wait in reception for your requisition. Thank you very much for coming.'

'Thank you, Mr Peters. I'll be in touch with you after you've received the consignment – if not before. And I won't forget to say "hello" to Scott.'

'And tell him he owes me two million lire! Bye, Mr Blake.'

The third meeting

Wrong

Arriving for his final meeting of the day, Humphrey Blake is led to the prospect's office.

'Do come in.'

'Thank you, Mr Saunders.'

'By the way. I'm sorry about last week. It was short notice, but it was unavoidable. These things happen.'

'What happened exactly?'

'You remember – I mentioned to you when I telephoned to cancel our meeting. I had a burst pipe at home; the whole house was flooded. I seem to recall you saying you had this problem last winter.'

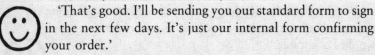

'Did I mention that to you? Oh yes. That's right.'

'Anyway. What was it you wanted to see me about?'

'A new product range that I think you'll like.'

A knock on the door.

'Oh, Barry. Come in – sit down.'

'Thanks.'

'Listen. I'd like you to meet Mr Blake of Corrugated Casings . . . Mr Blake, this is Barry Gwent, our production manager.'

'How do you do.' Shaking hands.

'Mr Blake's company supplies corrugated casings. Perhaps you'd like to give us an idea of your range, Mr Blake.'

'Certainly. Now where was I? Right. The capabilities of this range far exceed anything that we've had previously. And we've introduced a stock ordering procedure which will make it very easy for you people. If you've an ordinary micro you can just tap in to our central computer.'

'That sounds good.'

'It is good. All you need is to be on ASCII and you'll find there's no problem . . .'

Mr Saunders is distracted; he's wondering what on earth this ASCII can be. He's nodding away but isn't really listening. He doesn't want to ask and *appear ignorant* – especially as Gwent doesn't seem to be having any trouble with the jargon. (*'ASCII. Now what on earth is it: Aunt Sally's chocolate icing?'*)

He is now preoccupied with playing word games in his head in an effort to guess the answer. Mr Blake should have said what it is, he thinks. ('It's obviously significant. Still – never mind. I've missed most of what he's been saying now. I don't know how he expects me to buy when he doesn't spell out essential details of the package. Now – where am I supposed to meet Eileen for lunch today?')

Blake passes a magazine over to Gwent, pointing to a short paragraph that he wants him to look at: 'This is a write-up we've had about our new range. It mentions our factory and the loyalty of our staff, and how . . .'

Blake continues to speak to Gwent as he tries to read. Since he gets no response from Gwent he goes back to Saunders, who is still miles away (playing word games), and continues the conversation that he had hitherto been directing at the other man.

He then tries to reinterest Gwent who is still absorbed in reading, but it's difficult as there is no eye contact. Blake can't make him look up by using his name, because *he failed to pick this up* when they were introduced.

The telephone rings. 'Saunders speaking.'

'John. Have you got five minutes?'

'Yes, Karen. Come up. I'm in the middle of a meeting but you may find it interesting.'

'I'll be right there.'

Knock on the door. 'Come in, Karen. This is Mr Blake of Corinthian . . . sorry, Corrugated Casings. He's come over to show us some new products. Sit down.'

Gwent now finishes with the magazine and hands it back to the salesman.

Blake promptly proffers this to the new arrival. 'Yes – I was just showing er . . . er . . . the gentleman this recent editorial from the last issue of . . .'

He then looks over to Gwent and says to him: 'What did you think of the comments relating to the flexibility aspect?'

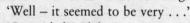

'Well – it seemed to be very . . .'

'One sided?' Blake interjects.

'Well, I suppose you might say that. I feel that the range is more suited to . . .'

'Large users?' Blake *interrupts* again.

'Well, maybe.'

'Yes I thought you might say that. But we do have very good payment terms. You could stagger the costs over a certain period.'

'Is it possible to have a . . .?'

'Trial?'

'Well, I was going to say, is it possible to have an idea of comparative costs under the different payment plans? But now that you mention it – that's an idea. A trial. That would solve the problem. We try a small amount and see how it goes down.'

'I'm sorry, but we've got no facility for a trial. The minimum order charge is 3000 pieces.' Having guessed the *wrong* ending, he has made the mood negative; a trial seems fair to the purchaser now, but the idea is being rejected by the very person who *suggested it*. 'It's not something that we do. I'm sure you'd be happy with the 3000 pieces if you took them. You've read the glowing report in the magazine.'

'Oh, yes' said Gwent. 'But it was written for the magazine by your public relations agency.'

'I think the best thing, Mr Blake' said Saunders, 'is for us to have a think about it. We'll let you know.'

'Very well. If you need any more information or reprints of that article, I'd be happy to send you some. Or if you want me to come and see you again.'

'Yes. We know where you are.'

'Well I hope you get your roof sorted out, Mr Saunders.'

'Er . . . I beg your pardon?'

'Your roof – hope it all works out.'

'Yes. Quite.'

When Blake leaves the three of them discuss his short-comings:

'That fellow is worrying. He shouldn't really be let loose.'

'Didn't ask any questions, for a start.'

'Didn't look you in the eye either. He had no feeling for our particular needs. Was only interested in prattling on, even when I was trying to read his PR blurb.'

'Now listen, Barry. You've got to help me out. It's driving me crazy. You're a computer man. What the deuce is ASCII?'

'Well, that's a coding system: American Standard Code for Information Interchange. What did you think it was – Aunt

Sally's chocolate icing?'

'Funny you should say that . . .!!'

Right

Arriving at the prospect's office.

'Do come in, Mr Blake.'

'Thank you, Mr Saunders.' Sits down as directed. 'Well. What happened with your burst pipe in the end? Was there much damage to your house?'

'Oh that. Don't ask. The place is in an absolute mess. We can only use one room. My wife's still distraught. The insurance company have been in. They've given the go-ahead to get the repairs done immediately. I've just got to find some decent builders now.'

'Oh I am sorry. I sympathize with you, having had the same problem last winter.'

'Yes. Did you get your repairs done satisfactorily. Any problems?'

'No, it was relatively smooth. We found a very competent firm of builders. They were used to dealing with repairs and disruption caused by flooding. They work really fast. As a matter of fact I think I've got their card in my wallet. If you're interested you could perhaps get an estimate from them.'

'That would be a great help. I'd really appreciate that.'

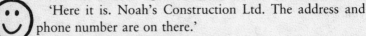

'Here it is. Noah's Construction Ltd. The address and phone number are on there.'

'Thank you. Now we'd better get down to what's brought you here. You said on the phone last week you've got some new products I might be interested in. Oh Sandra . . . coffee, Mr Blake? Right. Sandra, would you mind: two coffees . . .'

'Yes, we have some new ranges and I wanted an exploratory chat with you to see if we can help. Can I ask you: what volume of your business is done through mail order?'

'Well – we sent out over 20 000 consignments by mail order last year. That figure will probably increase in the next twelve months.'

'Oh. Are you expanding that side?'

'We've introduced a new item into the catalogue: portable fold-up ladders. They've only been available for three weeks, and I can tell you, in confidence, that we've already had orders for over 11 000. Quite staggering.'

'Do you actually have them in stock at the moment?'

'No. None at all. We're not taking delivery for another four weeks – from Geneva.'

'How will you be packaging them for despatch?'

'I'm not quite sure of that at the moment.'

'Now we have some special casings within our new range especially for bulky items such as ladders.'

'That sounds interesting. Actually that reminds me. I've asked our despatch supervisor to come and join us. He should be up shortly. Let me give him a ring in case he's forgotten. He's got problems at the moment. A lot of our goods have been damaged in transit through the packaging coming apart. Consequently he's facing a barrage of complaints from customers. Let me just try his extension.'

As he picks up the telephone there is a knock on the door.

'Come in. Oh, Barry – there you are. I was just ringing you, Barry, this is Humphrey Blake of Corrugated Casings.'

'Barry Gwent. How do you do, Mr Blake.' Handshake.

'Nice to meet you. Sorry, I didn't quite catch your name – Barry . . .?'

'Gwent.'

'Right. Thank you.' The two men sit down, and Blake hands a business card to the new arrival.

'Barry. Mr Blake was talking about a new range of casings. Perhaps you'd like to continue, Mr Blake.

'Yes. You were saying, Mr Saunders, that you might be interested in our casings for your successful portable ladders. Well, the range that we've just introduced is probably superior to anything that's around. Let me just show you this.'

Instantly produces looseleaf sheets (containing illustrations and dimensions) and passes one each to the two people present.

When they have both finished studying this and Blake can resume eye contact, he continues talking: 'As you can see, they're attractive and come in various dimensions. So their versatility is something that's being well received.'

'What's the situation for ordering?' Saunders asks.

'Well – I was just coming on to that. We've introduced a computerized stock ordering system for selected approved customers. If you have a micro, you can go on-line to our central computer in Basingstoke. The system runs on ASCII – a coding that stands for American Standard Code for Information Interchange. I don't know if that conforms to your present programme? Er – Mr Gwent. Have you an idea whether . . . ?'

'Oh, that's fine. We switched over to it about a year ago.'

'That's handy. In that case all of our range of products can be ordered through the central stock system. You'd get delivery very fast that way. And have all the current prices literally at your fingertips. So you'd be able to do your costings more accurately, and also shorten your delivery times to customers.'

'Do you have many companies in our line using this new range?'

'Oh certainly, Mr Gwent. You might like to read a few paragraphs of this press cutting from a trade magazine.' He passes the sheet over to Barry Gwent.

Looking at Mr Saunders: 'What other major bulky items are you sending out by mail order?'

'A lot of power tools. Home gym items – you know, exercise bikes, rowing machines, that sort of thing. Barry can give you more information on that. I think the report I had from him the other day showed that over – let me think – yes 60 per cent of our consignments are above 40 kg in weight.'

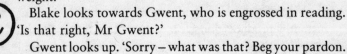

Blake looks towards Gwent, who is engrossed in reading. 'Is that right, Mr Gwent?'

Gwent looks up. 'Sorry – what was that? Beg your pardon.

I was just reading something else on this page. Very interesting.'

'Mr Saunders was just telling me that over 60 per cent of your consignments are over 40 kg.'

'Yes. That's right.'

Telephone rings. Saunders answers it: 'Saunders speaking.'

The voice on the other end: 'John – have you got five minutes?'

'Yes. Come up to my office, Karen. I'm in the middle of a meeting, but you'd probably find it of use.'

'I'll be right there.'

Knock on the door. 'Come in, Karen. This is Mr Blake. He's from Corrugated Casings. They've got some good products. Karen is our sales manager, by the way.'

'Hello – I'm Karen Carpenter.'

'Pleased to meet you, Miss Carpenter.'

'Let me see – Corrugated Casings. Didn't I read something about you recently? No – maybe I'm thinking of another company.'

'It probably was us. I was just showing Mr Gwent a recent press article. Was this it?'

'Yes – that's it. Do you mind if I take a look?'

'No – of course.'

Blake then directs himself to Gwent. 'What did you think of the comments in the article relating to the flexibility of the range?'

'Well – it seemed to be very complimentary. I feel that the range is more suited to companies like ourselves that need bespoke-type casings. It's certainly something that could help us.'

Blake to Gwent: 'I understand you're getting complaints from customers because the packaging is coming away from a lot of the goods.'

'Yes – too right. Karen's salespeople are taking a lot of flak at the moment.'

Karen looks up from reading. 'Yes – our products are good but we're getting unnecessary complaints. The goods are arriving damaged . . . the customers are holding up payment . . .'

 Blake directs his gaze to all three: 'What I think you should appreciate about this new range, and I know you will, is that all of the casings are burst resistant. And we give a guarantee too.'

'That sounds marvellous' says the sales manager. 'What are we talking about price-wise, Mr Blake? Have you discussed this with Barry and John?'

'No – not yet. If you take a look at this sheet, it gives you the various minimum orders and quantity discounts.'

After studying the sheet, Saunders says: 'It's more than we're paying at the moment. But then – mmm – I suppose we're talking about something that's different.'

 'Yes. Do you mind if I ask – Miss Carpenter – what do you do when the customers get goods that are damaged in transit?'

'Well – we send them a prepaid postage label to send the goods back.'

 'What happens then?'

'We ask them if they are prepared to wait for a replacement.'

 'What percentage agree to this?'

'Only about 30 per cent' Gwent interjects.

 'So as well as having to *pay* postage for the returned items, you also *lose* sales that were once firm orders' says Blake.

'Absolutely right' says the sales manager.

'And goodwill' says Saunders. 'We end up losing these customers for the future. They would probably have bought other products from the catalogue.'

 Blake: 'So if you paid a little more and asked us to handle your packaging requirements – wouldn't you say that your increased revenue, both present *and* future, would make the extra cost insignificant?'

Twenty minutes later after Blake had left, Saunders and Gwent discuss the meeting: 'You know, Barry, I think that fellow Blake sold his product well.'

'Well, actually John, I don't think he sold us anything. I think *we bought!*'

Questionnaire: have you developed ESP?

Check your empathy rating with this questionnaire. The answers and a scoring scale follow the questions.

1 What do you understand by the term 'empathy'? Is it:
  (a) The ability to change somebody else's mind
  (b) A shampoo
  (c) Seeing things as other people do and feeling with them
  (d) Not pushing too hard?

2 As you enter the client's (or your boss's) office, you see that she has just put down a bottle of tablets after swallowing two or more of these. She apologizes as she gets up to shake your hand. You note that the bottle is marked 'paracetamol'. Do you:
  (a) Assume everything is OK, since she hasn't brought up the subject in the first five minutes
  (b) Ask her if she's trying to end it all
  (c) Show concern and offer to reschedule the meeting if she's suffering discomfort
  (d) Tell her you know of a more powerful and effective analgesic?

3 If there is little to choose between different products in

terms of quality and price, studies show that people will choose on the basis of:

(a) Delivery
(b) Bribery
(c) The salesperson they'd most like to deal with
(d) Pressure from the secretary?

4 Tests show that we *speak* at roughly how many words per minute:

(a) 100–150
(b) 400–600
(c) 800–1000
(d) 1000–1200?

5 Tests show that we *think* at roughly how many words per minute:

(a) 800–1000
(b) 100–150
(c) 450–600
(d) 1000–1500?

6 You're with a prospective client; the secretary walks in with some coffee. She puts your cup on the edge of her boss's desk on top of some of his papers. Do you:

(a) Leave things as they are (after all, she didn't consider it a problem)
(b) Pretend you only drink spirits
(c) Remove it instantly and place it somewhere where it's not doing any harm, making sure the client sees your actions
(d) Finish the coffee and then move the empty cup away?

7 You're telephoning a prospective company. You find out from the switchboard who the relevant person is, and you're transferred directly to his extension. After you've enquired whether it's convenient to talk, he asks you to make it short because he's in a meeting. Do you:

(a) Get your pitch over with quickly, since you've

managed to seize an opportunity to talk to this busy man

(b) Tell him that you'll write to him

(c) Ask him lots of questions so that it will hopefully prolong the call in a natural manner

(d) Suggest that as he's busy you'd much prefer to call him later in the day or another day, if he would give you a specific time and date when he'll be free?

8 In the middle of a meeting with your client or prospect, his telephone rings. He apologizes and takes the call. While he's speaking, do you:

(a) Look at him and smile constantly so that he knows you respect the fact that he will have interruptions and that you are capable of remaining alert.

(b) Make a signal to him and sneak out to empty the bladder or chat to the secretary or receptionist

(c) Turn your gaze away from him and perhaps occupy yourself with some papers or make some notes

(d) Look impatient so that he knows you are busy too, and therefore hope it will make him hurry up?

9 The marketing director of your Australian operation is over here on a sales trip. He's accompanying you on a visit to one of your clients. When you fixed the meeting two weeks ago, your client mentioned he knew the town in Australia where your colleague hailed from. At the meeting your visitor says: 'I understand you know my home town.' Your client, after hesitation, responds with a weak 'yes' and changes the subject. It's obvious to you that he's forgotten and is trying to hide his embarrassment. What's more, you can almost see the wheels turning in his head as he desperately tries to remember; and he's not concentrating on what you're saying. Do you:

(a) Drop the subject — it's not important now

(b) Try and slip a note of paper to your client

(c) Subtly introduce the name in some way so that it's not obvious to both parties, e.g. 'Don's a bit of a legend in Kangahogan; he's been known to . . .'

(d) Say to your client: 'You do remember Don's home town, don't you?'

10 You're in a restaurant entertaining a client. The tables are very close together. At a certain point your discussion turns to something quite confidential and, because conversation has lagged on the table next to you, your client's manner suggests that he's hesitant to speak. Do you:

(a) Start speaking in a hushed voice and hope that he'll respond *sotto voce*

(b) Look sideways and stare at the people on the next table, and hope your body language will tell them to otherwise engage themselves

(c) Summon the waiter and ask him to turn up the muzak

(d) Try and change the subject for the moment until the coast is clear

(e) Ignore the silence on the next table and continue the discussion, but decide to boycott the restaurant in future because of the seating problem?

11 Your prospect keeps looking at his watch surreptitiously during your presentation. He doesn't think you've spotted this, but for the last thirty minutes it's been distracting you and preventing you giving your best. What do you do:

(a) Hurriedly bring your presentation to a close

(b) Just ignore it; it might be a nervous mannerism

(c) Stop talking at each point that he looks at his watch

(d) Ask him politely: 'How long have we got?' ?

12 A business prospect asks you to telephone him with a proposal (following your meeting) as soon as you have

formulated it. You telephone on Friday at 9.30 a.m. His secretary says he'll be out of a meeting at around 4 p.m., and warns you that he'll be leaving at 4.30 to visit somebody in hospital. Do you:

(a) Leave the details with the secretary
(b) Call him at the hospital
(c) Call him at 4.25 p.m.
(d) Call him on Monday
(e) Call him at 4 p.m.?

13 You promise a client that the next time you meet you'll bring him a rare copy of an early Superman comic for his son. You forget this the next time you meet at his office. However, as you are leaving and walking past the security desk towards the revolving doors, you suddenly remember. Do you:

(a) Forget it: assume he's forgotten, since there was no mention of it (besides, you'd like to hang on to it; could be worth something, come to think of it)
(b) Make sure you remember it the next time you see him
(c) Telephone him from the security desk and say that you haven't forgotten about it and you'll get it to him very soon
(d) To save face, tell him the next time you meet that it's been stolen?

14 Your red felt-tip pen has leaked and there's a lot of ink showing down the front of your shirt. As you enter the prospect's office, your mind is on how to conceal this. Do you:

(a) Hope he or she will not notice
(b) Keep your arms folded at all times, and ask for a straw if you're offered coffee
(c) Tell him at the outset as soon as you arrive what's happened, and make fun of your carelessness
(d) Cancel the meeting?

15 The golden rule for effective presentation and maximizing attention is (fill in the blanks):
   Say what – – – – Going – – – – – .
   Say – – .
   Say – – – – you – – – – .

16 After a long meeting with the prospect, during which he insisted on covering all the nitty-gritty in your literature and the fine print, he agrees to a trial order. Your order form contains many terms and conditions. To close the sale, do you:
   (a) Produce the order form quickly and go through each item with him
   (b) Ask him to confirm the order in writing (possibly their own purchase order), preferably for you to take with you. You can then send the official form on to him with an acknowledgement letter.
   (c) Make an exception with this client and accept a verbal handshake agreement
   (d) Ask for payment in advance (used £5 notes)?

17 You're introduced to three new people, but you miss one of the names. What do you do:
   (a) Not worry – two out of three isn't bad
   (b) Ask him: 'Sorry – I didn't catch your name'
   (c) Guess
   (d) Ask one of the other two people his name when he's distracted?

18 The secretary walks into her boss's office during the meeting you're having with him, and says: 'Mr Scott said could you give him a buzz on 421 within the next ten minutes. He said it's urgent and he'll be going out soon.' Do you:
   (a) Accelerate your talk so as to be finished within 7–8 minutes

(b) Say to the client that there is no way you can be expected to finish your presentation in a few minutes, and that you hadn't realized there'd be such a time constraint

(c) Politely suggest that he may like to sort that out now while you occupy yourself with some paperwork

(d) Wait for him to say something, and if he doesn't just carry on as normal?

19 Do you appreciate the meaning of 'psycholinguistics'? Is it:
(a) An aerobic exercise from California
(b) The study of how celluloid thrillers affect the mind
(c) How certain words affect our minds and emotions?

20 You have to write to a prospect following a meeting in which you were negotiating on price. He wants from you a deal involving quantity discount, giving a unit price of £5.50 instead of the £6.20 you have quoted at the meeting. You have decided that £5.86 is the lowest you can drop to. How is your letter phrased:
(a) '. . . unfortunately £5.86 is the best price we can do for you at the moment . . .'
(b) '. . . so I'm afraid to have to tell you that the lowest figure we're able to offer would be £5.86 . . .'
(c) '. . . we're happy to say that we'll work with you on a rate of £5.86, and there may be scope to reduce that figure if volume increases; we can discuss . . .'
(d) '. . . you said at the meeting that it would be impossible for you to do business with us unless we could drop to £5.50 at least . . .'?

21 When you're with clients and you hand them material to look at, do you:
(a) Decide to make it easy for them by giving them a running commentary as they're reading
(b) Ask them to wake you up when they've finished

(c) Remain silent?

22 Do you appreciate the timely value of silence in any selling situation? If you do, then correctly fill in the blanks for this ancient proverb:

Better to keep your – – – – shut and be *thought* a – – – –, than to – – – – it and remove all – – – – –!

23 Many so-called objections are not in fact so. When you get inside the mind of the other person, then you often find that the *genuine* ones are simply:
   (a) Statements made by the prospect to make him feel good about himself
   (b) Demands for reassurance
   (c) Questions to prolong the meeting because he wants to look busy in front of his colleagues.

24 You're going on holiday to Tuscany this year. You're moving house in the autumn. During your conversation with a prospect, he reveals that he himself is off to Florence the next weekend. When he returns from holiday, he is away for a further two weeks because he is moving house. He suggests you contact him again after two months when the dust has settled. You don't rate yourself as having a good memory, but there are two pieces of information which you must have registered and should not fail to use when you meet this person again. Which two?
   (a) You remember that the prospect was a man
   (b) You remember he was going to Florence the last time you met
   (c) You remember he wore glasses
   (d) You remember he was moving house.

25 The following is a true story.
   Tony Wright left his house at the same time every morning. He walked to the underground station where

he caught a crowded train that took him in to the City. The yuppie revolution ensured that the twenty minute journey was invariably spent standing, huddled up with others trying to capitalize on every square inch of space.

Whilst he was aware of the importance of eye contact, he didn't realize that this extended to observing fellow travellers at close quarters. The dishevelled man standing next to him obviously did. Wright decided that this fellow staring at him suspiciously deserved a rebuff. So he turned a half-circle and was faced with a much better proposition in the form of a very pretty brunette.

At the next station the train ground to a severe halt and a few passengers fell about, including the man with the staring eyes. He fell on Tony Wright and held on to what appeared to be the lapels of his jacket. It was almost deliberate, concluded Wright, as he fixed a disapproving stare at the man, who seemed to be trying now to wade through the crowded train towards the doors.

Tony Wright brushed an imaginary fleck of dirt off his shoulder and flattened his lapels. As he was patting his jacket he subconsciously registered that the normal bulge of his inside pocket was not there. His wallet. It had gone.

His thoughts immediately turned to the man, who was frantically trying to get to the doors. Of course. That's what he was up to. 'Stop him. Stop him. Thief' he shouted, as faces looked up from newspapers in complete surprise. The thief was just getting off the train, and the automatic doors had started to close. Wright leapt to the doors and just about managed to grab the culprit's tie as the doors closed.

'Stop the train – stop the train!' Wright shouted, but it started moving. He held on to the tie. The thief started waving his arms and cursing, and was yanked along as the train was moving. His head was banging along the side of the doors and blood started to appear all over his face. Some of the passengers screamed. 'Let him go' they

shouted at Wright, but he hung on to the man's tie as the train sped along. 'He's got my wallet' snarled Wright, as he justified his iron-like grip on the tie. The thief was looking in a bad way as blood poured from everywhere. 'We're going in the tunnel now!' somebody shouted in horror, and luckily for the thief the tie snapped in Wright's hands. The bloodstained man was left staggering on the platform.

Wright cursed himself. 'I nearly had him' he thought. The train pulled up at the next station and Wright got out. He had a client meeting that morning, but there was no possibility of attending that. His hands were grazed and bloodstained. He walked to the telephone booth, and instantly recalled the telephone number of his clients using his unique memory system. He felt rather pleased with himself at being able to remember the number. He spoke to the clients, explained what had happened, and said that he was on his way to his office now and would give them a call to reschedule after checking with his diary.

He got a taxi and, after proudly recounting the story to an inquisitive taxi driver, eventually arrived at his destination. He walked up the stairs and entered his office, where he was greeted by his shocked secretary.

'Are you all right, Mr Wright? What on earth has happened to you?'

'Oh – nothing. Don't worry. I've got to reschedule another meeting now with Hi Tech Systems: could you get my diary.'

'Oh by the way, Mr Wright. Your wife called.'

'Did she leave any message?'

'Yes. She said . . .'

What was the message from his wife? (The answer is worth 10 points.)

Answers

1 (a) 0
  (b) −5
  (c) +10. Interestingly, the Greek origin of the word means 'to feel pain with'.
  (d) 0

2 (a) +1. Most people wouldn't.
  (b) −5
  (c) +5. More likely than not she won't be able to give you worthwhile attention. Her mind will be on how to shorten the meeting.
  (d) +2

3 (a) +1
  (b) 0
  (c) +5. *You* provide the added value.
  (d) +1

4 (a) +5. Right answer.
  (b) 0
  (c) −2
  (d) −5

5 (a) +1
  (b) −2

(c) +5. Right answer. Remember: we can think at roughly four times the rate at which somebody is speaking. Small wonder that we have to work hard to detect and prevent loss of attention from our audience.

(d) 0

6 (a) 0. It isn't her problem.

(b) 0

(c) +5. He can concentrate on your presentation now instead of worrying about his papers.

(d) +1

7 (a) +1

(b) +1

(c) −5. He hasn't got the time or inclination right now. He's distracted; he's got people with him and he's keeping them waiting. If you're not careful and you push it, he'll impress the people in his office by the assertive act of getting rid of you.

(d) +5. You're more likely to have a better chance of achieving your goal.

8 (a) −2. Give him some breathing space. Don't stare at him. And what are you grinning at anyway? You can't hear the conversation.

(b) −4

(c) +5. You're making him feel comfortable now. It's in your interest; he's secretly thanking you for it. What empathy.

(d) −5

9 (a) 0

(b) +1

(c) +5. You've embarrassed neither of the parties. You've been subtle; they probably don't know what you've been trying to do. Even if your client guesses, he can't be sure. Besides, he's now more comfortable; he can engage in natural conversation.

(d) −5. Don't make him lose face.

10 (a) +2
    (b) +1
    (c) −4
    (d) +5
    (e) −5. Doesn't help you for the moment. Bad seating is a common fault in many restaurants and hotels. Best to make sure you choose a good table in the first place if you're discussing business.

11 (a) 0
    (b) +1
    (c) −1
    (d) +5. You should find out the real problem this way.

12 (a) −3
    (b) −10
    (c) −5
    (d) +5. You should get a better reception. Also he's got an uninterrupted working week to concentrate on it, rather than a weekend to dilute its impact.
    (e) −2. Will he be in the mood?

13 (a) −5
    (b) +1. There might not now be a next time.
    (c) +10. No time like the present. He'd been disturbed during the meeting by your empty promise. He'd began to doubt your sincerity.
    (d) −10

14 (a) −5. The distraction for the client would be too great. He'd be wondering if it was your bullet-proof vest that had failed; or was it clumsiness with a tomato ketchup bottle? But more importantly – he'd be dying

to know if *you* knew about the stain. Total
distraction.

(b) −4

(c) +5. At least he knows that *you* know. Also there's an
explanation; you're not just a slob!

(d) 0. Have you really got precious time to be able to do
this?

15 Say what you're going to say.
Say it.
Say what you said.
(+5 points for correct answer)

16 (a) −2. If he's that pedantic it may make him change his
mind. He may want to hold off and study it carefully.

(b) +5. He's committed himself in his own mind now.

(c) −5

(d) 0

17 (a) −1. No excuse. Could be the most important member of the group.

(b) +5. Now you're talking.

(c) −10. Worse than no name − the *wrong* name!

(d) +2

18 (a) −5

(b) +2. If you're going to phrase it this way, be polite.

(c) +5. At least he'll be able to concentrate on you now.

(d) −1. He may spring a 'thank you for coming' abruptly
after five minutes (and you haven't finished).

19 (a) −4

(b) −5. You're thinking of Hitchcock.

(c) +5

20 (a) −4. 'Unfortunately . . .': you're planting negative
vibes in the other person's mind. Why?

(b) −5. 'So I'm afraid . . .': ugh!

(c) +5. 'We're happy to say . . .': you've turned negative vibes into positive ones. Bravo! And you're offering exactly the *same* deal.

(d) −10. Don't remind him of this. He probably forgot that he even said it.

21 (a) −4. Can you really concentrate on two things at once?

(b) −5

(c) +5

22 Better to keep your mouth shut and be *thought* a fool, than to open it and remove all doubt!
(+5 points for correct answer)

23 (a) 0

(b) +5

(c) −3. This type does exist, beyond a doubt. But we're talking about people with genuine intentions of buying.

24 (a) −5

(b) +5

(c) −4

(d) +5. If you can't programme your mind to remember (b) and (d), which are common to you both, then there's no hope.

25 'Yes. *She said you left your wallet on the dining room table.*'
(You deserve +10 points. Wasn't you, was it?)

Scoring scale

130 to 140	This book must have done you some good. Empathy is oozing out of you.
100 to 129	You're developing ESP by the minute.
75 to 99	Nearly there.

50 to 74	A few weak areas that need working on.
21 to 49	Come on – get inside the mind.
5 to 20	Please read the book again.
– 100 to 4	*Don't answer any more questions without checking with your solicitor!*

A Selected List of Non-Fiction Available from Mandarin

While every effort is made to keep prices low, it is sometimes necessary to increase prices at short notice. Mandarin Paperbacks reserves the right to show new retail prices on covers which may differ from those previously advertised in the text or elsewhere.

The prices shown below were correct at the time of going to press.

☐	7493 0109 0	**The Warrior Queens**	Antonia Fraser	£4.99
☐	7493 0108 2	**Mary Queen of Scots**	Antonia Fraser	£5.99
☐	7493 0010 8	**Cromwell**	Antonia Fraser	£7.50
☐	7493 0106 6	**The Weaker Vessel**	Antonia Fraser	£5.99
☐	7493 0014 0	**The Demon Drink**	Jancis Robinson	£4.99
☐	7493 0016 7	**Vietnam – The 10,000 Day War**	Michael Maclear	£3.99
☐	7493 0061 2	**Voyager**	Yeager/Rutan	£3.99
☐	7493 0113 9	**Peggy Ashcroft**	Michael Billington	£3.99
☐	7493 0177 5	**The Troubles**	Mick O'Connor	£4.99
☐	7493 0004 3	**South Africa**	Graham Leach	£3.99
☐	7493 0254 2	**Families and How to Survive Them**	Creese/Skynner	£5.99
☐	7493 0060 4	**The Fashion Conspiracy**	Nicolas Coleridge	£3.99
☐	7493 0179 1	**The Tao of Pooh**	Benjamin Hoff	£2.99
☐	7493 0000 0	**Moonwalk**	Michael Jackson	£2.99

All these books are available at your bookshop or newsagent, or can be ordered direct from the publisher. Just tick the titles you want and fill in the form below.

Mandarin Paperbacks, Cash Sales Department, PO Box 11, Falmouth, Cornwall TR10 9EN.

Please send cheque or postal order, no currency, for purchase price quoted and allow the following for postage and packing:

UK   80p for the first book, 20p for each additional book ordered to a maximum charge of £2.00.

BFPO   80p for the first book, 20p for each additional book.

Overseas   £1.50 for the first book, £1.00 for the second and 30p for each additional book
including Eire thereafter.

NAME (Block letters) ....

ADDRESS ....

....

....